Epiphany

Aids for Interpreting
the Lessons of the Church Year

Epiphany

Charles Carlston

Elizabeth Achtemeier, series editor

Series B

FORTRESS PRESS   Philadelphia

Third printing 1987

———————

Library of Congress Cataloging in Publication Data

Carlston, Charles E.
  Epiphany, series B.

  (Proclamation 3)
  1. Bible—Homiletical use. 2. Bible—Liturgical lessons, English. 3. Epiphany season. I. Title.
II. Series.
BS534.5.C37 1984   220.6   84–6012
ISBN 0–8006–4102–7

———————

3299J87   Printed in the United States of America   1–4102

Contents

Series Foreword

Proclamation 3 is an entirely new aid for preaching from the three-year ecumenical lectionary. In outward appearance this new series is similar to *Proclamation: Aids for Interpreting the Lessons of the Church Year* and *Proclamation 2*. But *Proclamation 3* has a new content as well as a new purpose.

First, there is only one author for each of the twenty-eight volumes of *Proclamation 3*. This means that each author handles both the exegesis and the exposition of the stated texts, thus eliminating the possibility of disparity between scholarly apprehension and homiletical application of the appointed lessons. While every effort was made in *Proclamation: Aids* and in *Proclamation 2* to avoid such disparity, it tended to creep in occasionally. *Proclamation 3* corrects that tendency.

Second, *Proclamation 3* is directed primarily at homiletical interpretation of the stated lessons. We have again assembled the finest biblical scholars and preachers available to write for the series; now, however, they bring their skills to us not primarily as exegetes, but as interpreters of the Word of God. Exegetical material is still presented—sometimes at length—but, most important, here it is also applied; the texts are interpreted and expounded homiletically for the church and society of our day. In this new series scholars become preachers. They no longer stand back from the biblical text and just discuss it objectively. They engage it—as the Word of God for the worshiping community. The reader therefore will not find here the divisions between "exegesis" and "homiletical interpretation" that were marked off in the two earlier series. In *Proclamation 3* the work of the pulpit is the context and goal of all that is written.

There is still some slight diversity between the several lections and calendars of the various denominations. In an effort to overcome such diversity, the North American Committee on a Common Lectionary issued an experimental "consensus lectionary" *(The Common Lectionary)*, which is now being tried out in some congregations and which will be further altered at the end of a three-year period. When

7

the final form of that lectionary appears, *Proclamation* will take account of it. In the meantime, *Proclamation 3* deals with those texts that are used by *most* denominations on any given Sunday. It also continues to use the Lutheran numbering of the Sundays "after Pentecost." But Episcopalians and Roman Catholics will find most of their stated propers dealt with under this numbering.

Each author writes on three lessons for each Sunday, but no one method of combining the appointed lessons has been imposed upon the writers. The texts are sometimes treated separately, sometimes together—according to the author's own understanding of the texts' relationships and messages. The authors interpret the appointed texts as these texts have spoken to them.

Charles E. Carlston is Norris Professor of New Testament Interpretation at Andover Newton Theological School. Educated at Harvard and at Fuller Theological Seminary, he is the author of *The Parables of the Triple Tradition* and of numerous scholarly articles. He served Presbyterian churches in Iowa and has taught at the University of Dubuque, the University of Iowa, and the Kirchliche Hochschule in West Berlin. He and his wife have five children.

ELIZABETH ACHTEMEIER

The Epiphany of Our Lord

Lutheran	Roman Catholic	Episcopal	Pres/UCC/Chr	Meth/COCU
Isa. 60.1–6	Isa. 60.1–6	Isa. 60:1–6, 9	Isa. 60:1–6	Isa. 60:1–6
Eph. 3:2–21	Eph. 3:2–3, 5–6	Eph. 3:1–12	Eph. 3:1–6	Eph. 3:1–12
Matt. 2:1–12	Matt. 2:1–12	Matt. 2:1–12	Matt. 2:1–12	Matt. 2:1–12

FIRST LESSON: ISAIAH 60:1–6

It is generally recognized that the last part of the Book of Isaiah consists of very disparate materials, mostly from the latter half of the sixth century B.C., when some had returned from exile (537) but the new Temple had not yet been consecrated. Of this section ("Trito-Isaiah") chapters 60–62 form the nucleus. The hopes of chapter 54 seem in chapter 60 to be in imminent process of being fulfilled; the mood is positive throughout, salvation (not, as often in the prophets, salvation and judgment together) forming the central emphasis. This is the more striking in that chapters 60–62 are set between two laments, chapters 59 and 63f., the former so savage an indictment of the people of God that Paul can quote it in support of his argument for universal sinfulness (cf. 59:7–8 with Rom. 3:15–17), the latter a vivid description of the winepress of God's fury (63:3; cf. Rev. 19:15).

Our passage offers to the wretched returnees in Jerusalem the promise that God still has the last word: "Arise, shine; for your light has come, and the glory of the Lord has risen upon you." These words, like the opening words of the following chapter (61:1), doubtless reflect, on the individual level, the prophet's own call; they are still useful as an expression of how Christians understand their own vocations in the world. On the communal level, they are used at Epiphany because Christians recognize in them a profound expression of the note of fulfillment they see in the coming of the Christ. "The hopes and fears of all the years"—and of nations and kings—are met in his birth.

Perhaps the central note in the passage is the insistence (vv. 3, 6, 9) that the light comes to all the nations, and they to the light. That

9

Midian, Ephah, and Sheba are mentioned by name (v. 6) doubtless shows that all of Abraham's descendants (cf. Gen. 25:1–4) are included in the promise. But the stress is only partially on the subjection of the nations; it also includes their sharing in the light. Our contemporary message to a broken world cannot be simply on the role reversal of which prophets in every age so gladly speak; we must also proclaim the establishing of justice, the overcoming of darkness, and the spreading of the light.

The symbol of light and darkness seems to be almost primordial in human history. Used by poets and lovers, by statesmen and administrators, by parents and preachers in a thousand cultures, it seems to speak to some need almost too deep to be acknowledged. And if one of the functions of art, symbol, and rhetoric is to attach emotion to information, then this passage should fittingly be sung, not merely read. Its striking cadences, particularly vv. 1–2, represent a call to depths where no sinner is abandoned, no saint secure, no promise beyond hope of realization. Perhaps no greater challenge exists for the modern preacher than to sort out, on every level from the individual to the multinational, the various elements of judgment and grace in the promise of these few verses (and the very similar ones forming the beginning of chapter 61).

SECOND LESSON: EPHESIANS 3:2–21

This long section is clearly related to Col. 1:24–27, where also the theme of Paul's suffering and service for the church is stressed. Our passage is in two parts—vv. 2–12, Paul's stewardship of the mystery revealed to him, and vv. 13–21, his intercession and prayer for the church. (V. 1 is a mere torso, though it includes the theme of the section as a whole, Paul's suffering for the Gentiles.)

Several terms in the first part are striking. In v. 3 we have "mystery" (as always in Ephesians, Paul's "stewardship" v. 2, is a reference to the revealed mystery, not to his "office"), "made known," and "revealed." More in keeping with the modern temper, no doubt, would be the thought that justice, equity, and good sense combined to convince Paul that Jews and Gentiles ought not to discriminate in society or church. But a church that has "worship experiences" (instead of worshiping God) is comparatively helpless in the face of profound hostilities of the kind reflected here. So the author (probably not Paul himself) is not ashamed to speak of Paul's "insight" (v. 4), but the insight rests on the revealing by the Spirit "to (God's) holy apostles and prophets" (v. 5, a very unPauline phrase) a fact that is true regardless of how the Ephesians (or any others) happen to feel about it. In this life we determine who our "heirs" shall be, but in the inheriting of the gospel (vv. 6–7) God has retained that privilege. It is ours to attest—but not to dispense!

It is important to be cautious in this matter. Christians with revelations—whether lay or clerical—rightly make us very uncomfortable. So it should be noted that the revelation is by the Spirit, to the church, for a wider (not a narrower) gospel, long planned by God (see v. 9), and so on. It might also be noted that there is, according to the nearly unanimous understanding of the church universal, a basic difference between Paul's authority and ours.

In v. 6 three words begin with *syn-* (together), though we cannot so translate them in English. The basic truth of the unity of Jew and Gentile, however, is by no means automatic. It is in the gospel. That means that the church must not only preach it; it must find ways of representing it before the world. As one commentator has put it, "The church is the model of reconciliation for the world." Christians' insistence on their social position over acceptance of the gospel's demands in many of the world's trouble spots—Lebanon, Northern Ireland, and South Africa come immediately to mind—is not, consequently, a mere religious difference, a "squabble of monks." It is a denial before an unbelieving world of the truth here revealed.

Another central emphasis in this section is the centrality of grace. Paul was called, empowered by the Spirit (not qualified by talent or training), though he was "the very least of all the saints"—in the moral race not part of the majority but last of all (vv. 2, 7, 8)! Because his message has to do with "the unsearchable riches of Christ," not with his own experience, he is comparatively unconcerned about his own effectiveness. "God, who created all things," "the manifold wisdom of God," "the eternal purpose . . . realized in Christ Jesus"—these alone are his concern.

The "heavenly powers" (in the ancient world, a symbol of the meaninglessness of life) are here confronted, not with the church, but with the plan of God made known through the church (v. 10). A helpful exercise might be to go through this whole passage to see how often God or words depicting the activity of God are mentioned. In a fragmented world—the kind we live in—the preacher's opinions, however cogently argued or vehemently affirmed, are simply not adequate to prevent the people from losing heart; access to God alone can meet that need (vv. 12–13).

"Paul" now turns to prayer, a prayer filled with theological content as well as earnestness and feeling. He "bows the knee" (an archaic biblical expression; prayer was ordinarily standing) to the "Father" for the "family." (In Greek, as in English, the word play is clear: *patera/patria*.) The emphasis on creation, rather than redemption, in v. 14 suggests that the term *every family* is rhetorical for *all human beings*.

The petition itself is threefold (vv. 17, 18, 19): to be strengthened within, that Christ might dwell within, that they might comprehend the incomprehensible. Note that none of this is automatic, as in both ancient and modern gnosticisms. Christ dwells through faith; love is not completely natural, even for the believer.

Finally, it should be noted throughout this section how frequently the church is mentioned or implied. The religious fervor of this passage suggests the term *mysticism,* but if by that word we intend something like the flight of the Alone to the Alone, it is absent here. The church does not control or dispense Christ. But it is in the church, with all the saints, that we encounter the one who by both creation and redemption has made us one with himself and with one another.

GOSPEL: MATTHEW 2:1–12

The first two chapters of Matthew set forth a large number of Matthean themes, particularly in Christology. In chapter 1 Jesus is variously shown to be Messiah, Son of David (so also Joseph), Son of Abraham, Savior, Emmanuel (cf. 28:20), the virgin-born son of Mary, the fulfiller of prophecy. In chapter 2 some of these themes are repeated, and special emphasis is given to the fact that the very town of Jesus' birth is predicted in Scripture (2:5f.). Of particular importance here is the title King of the Jews (2:2; cf. 27:29, 37, 42), which establishes the terms of the hostility between the child and Herod the king (2:1).

If 2:12 contains an allusion to the man of God in 1 Kings 13:9f., every one of the five subsections in chapter 2 (1–6, 7–12, 13–15, 16–18, 19–23) ends with a scriptural reference. None of the references are particularly exact or cited with careful regard for their context (as some wag has said of Stendahl's *The School of St. Matthew,* "If it was a school, it wasn't a very good one!''), but the mode of citation and interpretation is common first-century practice. Unless we wish to absolutize the particular exegetical methods in vogue in our day, the right question to ask is, What lay behind the use actually made of the texts? In our case, the answers are not hard to find.

The first section of chapter 2—vv. 1–6—includes two important motifs. The first is the struggle between Herod and the newborn king. (The controversy between Pharaoh and Moses is here, as in Heb. 3:1–6, moved to an even higher plane; Jesus is like Moses but more than Moses.) The second is that provided by the "wise men." (The text does not say that they were kings, nor that there were three of them, nor that one was black, nor that Matthew knew their names. Christmas pageants tell the truth; they do not convey facts.) Many ancient commentators were deeply troubled by the clear indication that these "Chaldeans" were astrologers; in their day, as in ours, astrology was rightly judged to be dangerous folly. It should perhaps be pointed out, however, that about all their pseudoscience told them was that a Jewish king had been born; the Scripture was needed to tell them where. (Then, somewhat inconsistently, they follow the star to the very house, which Luther explained by suggesting that they followed a special star, created for the purpose, which hovered only a few feet above the housetops!) We do not think in the same cosmological terms. But the patristic (and biblical) notion that Christ has set us free from every cosmic power that would thwart our freedom is a very powerful and useful one.

The hypocritical Herod (2:7f.) here sets himself against the Lord's anointed, but to no avail. The counterkings (the parallels in Pss. 45:7–9; 72:10, 15; Song of Sol. 3:6f.; Isa. 49:7; 60:3, 6, 10 reflect the theme of royalty), guided by the star (cf. the messianic prophecy in Num. 24:17, significant in both Qumran, CD vii. 19, and the second century revolt of Bar Cochba), find the child and "worship" him (vv. 2, 11—the word is used ten times in Matthew with reference to Jesus) before returning safely to their own home.

In this whole section, in fact, the hand of God may be seen at work. An angel warns them (2:12), just as Joseph is warned throughout chapters 1–2. (See 1:20; 2:13, 22.) Herod may try his worst, but the Scripture will be fulfilled and the child will survive to save his people. One theme commonly overlooked in the dramatic power of the several episodes in this section is the note in 2:10 that the wise men "rejoiced exceedingly with great joy" when they arrived at Jesus' house. (The RSV is a good literal translation of the very strong Greek phrase.)

The thematic connection between this reading and the others for this Sunday is clearly God's will to save the nations. Jesus is rejected by the Jewish king but acknowledged as King of the Jews by strangers from the East. The text even points out that Jesus' coming troubled not only Herod but the whole city. (A modern counterpart might be something like "Solzhenitsyn's work shook Moscow to its foundations" or "Martin Luther King changed Washington forever." Cities, then as now, are symbols of power as well as aggregates of human beings.) We know that Jerusalem, age-old city of God, will never be the same again. What has changed is that the saving purpose of God is now unequivocally extended beyond the Holy City, beyond the people it represents, to the whole world. The book begins, as it will end (28:19), with this clear note. The King of the Jews, as Son of God, becomes Savior of the world.

The Baptism of Our Lord
The First Sunday After the Epiphany

Lutheran	Roman Catholic	Episcopal	Pres/UCC/Chr	Meth/COCU
Isa. 42:1–7	Isa. 42:1–4, 6–7	Isa. 42:1–9	Isa. 61:1–4	Isa. 42:1–9
Acts 10:34–38	Acts 10:34–38	Acts 10:34–38	Acts 11:4–18	Acts 10:34–38
Mark 1:4–11	Mark 1:7–11	Mark 1:7–11	Mark 1:4–11	Mark 1:4–11

FIRST LESSON: ISAIAH 42:1–9

Our text includes the first two of the famous "Servant Songs" of Second Isaiah (42:1–4; 42:5–9; 49:1–6; 49:7–13; 50:4–9; 50:10–11; 52:13—53:12). (A few of the passages are occasionally combined with the contiguous ones, so not all studies count seven in all.) Christians read them—especially the first and last—in terms of their fulfillment in Jesus Christ, a practice that can be traced back at least to the end of the first century (Matt. 8:17; 12:18–21; Luke 2:32; 22:37; John 12:38; Acts 8.32–33, 13.47, 1 Pet. 2.22–25; Rev. 7.16–17) and possibly somewhat earlier.

Historically, it is quite improbable that the writer(s) of these poems intended a single, still future, personal reference. But we have learned little in the last generation of biblical scholarship if we assume that the original historical reference of any biblical text exhausts all legitimate interpretive possibilities. The critical question in all promise-and-fulfillment texts is whether and how the hopes and longings expressed in the text are fulfilled in subsequent history—for Christians, in the people of God and in Jesus Christ, God's Son.

With this functional question in mind, we turn to the details, both positive and negative. The servant is one sustained, chosen, and approved by God, empowered by the Spirit, sent to "bring forth," to establish "justice" (vv. 1, 3, 4). With reference to the Gentiles, this implies both judgment on their gods and their doings and, at the same time, release from the harsher aspects of that judgment, particularly their exclusion from the Lord's salvation. (Cf. also 49:6.) For such news the people are waiting (v. 4; cf. 51:5–6). Christian theology at its best has always, like this song, included both justice and judgment while understanding both only in the context of God's gracious plan to save.

That the servant does not "lift up his voice" (v. 2) may reflect the ancient Oriental custom in which a new king on his accession has the laws reproclaimed publicly; if so, the text envisions a different kind of king. Hints of the servant's compassion for others, especially the needy (v. 3), are combined with a suggestion of his own suffering and victory over it (v. 4). The carefully worked out poetry of this passage is evident in the verbal connections between v. 3 and v. 4: bruise/burning/justice and burn dimly/be bruised/establish justice. (The RSV obscures the parallelism.)

The second song (vv. 5–9) is more difficult and the allusions obscure. The moving and sonorous affirmations of v. 5 define the nature of the God who calls: He is Creator of the universe and of all human beings. On this rests his will to save—not by tolerance of all customs or religions (v. 8!)—but by special concern for the needy: the blind, the imprisoned, and those who walk in darkness (v. 7). (It might be an interesting exercise to try to list the various contemporary understandings of God that are excluded by these half-dozen critical elements, not to turn a sermon into some kind of harangue, but simply to note how badly we need the guidance of both testaments in developing a working understanding of God's nature and purpose.)

And so the preacher is brought back to our first question: How do we know who the servant is? In our text many ambiguities remain. But as Christians we recognize Jesus Christ as the servant of Second Isaiah and the one who "came not to be served but to serve" (Mark 10:45). This functional definition of the servant then carries with it a profound challenge to those who claim membership in the servant-people of God: Are we a light to the nations, a source of hope for those suffering under either natural or man-made handicaps (v. 7), a candle in the darkness of our twentieth-century world?

SECOND LESSON: ACTS 10:34–38

This text too deals with the range of God's concern for the world, a significant motif in Luke (see 2:30–32; 3:38; 7:1–10; 10:29–37; 17:11–19; 24:47) as well as elsewhere in Acts (1:8; chap. 2; chap. 8; etc.).

Yet Acts 10 occupies a special place in this scheme, since the acceptability of the Gentiles is here confirmed in at least four ways: (1) by Peter's vision (10:9–16); (2) by Peter's conversion through this vision (10:28); (3) by the vision sent to Cornelius, which puts him in touch with Peter (10:30–33); and (4) by the descent of the Spirit upon Cornelius, his relatives, and his close friends (10:24, 44f.). Naturally, Luke cannot stress the church's resistance to this development (cf. Galatians); but he spells out enough of it to heighten the drama.

Our text (10:34–38) is the first part of Peter's reply to Cornelius, a section containing four significant elements: (1) vv. 34–35, the setting and enunciation of the general principle, the acceptability of all; (2) vv. 36–41, the ministry of Jesus and the apostolic witness; (3) v. 43a, the scriptural proof; and (4) vv. 42–43, the call to repentance. The pattern is a common one in the early speeches in Acts.

V. 34 begins in solemn fashion: "Peter opened his mouth and said: 'Truly . . .'"; the phrases, so biblically nuanced, show the importance of what is to follow, in this case the teaching that God "is no respector of persons," an unusually widespread biblical emphasis (Deut. 10:17; Rom. 2:11; Eph. 6:9; Col. 3:25; 1 Pet. 1:17; cf. Jas. 2:1, 9; etc.).

Nowhere in the Bible, however, is universal acceptability stressed without some kind of definition. In v. 35 Luke carefully notes that they are acceptable to God who "fear him and do what is right." The principle is that God does not discriminate unjustly.

In v. 36 the "word," (as in 13:26) is the Christian word of salvation. It is immediately connected (again as in 13:26) with both Christ and the Scriptures. It is a specific word: the good news is "peace through Jesus Christ." The title, "Lord of all," originally a pagan predicate of God, is here personal: Lord of all people, that is, of both Jews and Gentiles.

In v. 37, as in 13:24, Jesus' ministry begins, not with his birth, but with the ministry of John the Baptist. Luke's primary emphasis is not, like John's, on the incarnation, nor, like Paul's and Mark's, on Jesus' saving death; it is rather on Jesus' ministry as a whole.

The theme of Jesus as the Anointed One (v. 38; see also 17:3; 18:28; 24:24; 26:23; etc.) is here spelled out in language strongly reminiscent of Isa. 61:1, already used by Luke (4:18) as the basis of Jesus' ministry. Since this and similar Isaianic texts are also alluded to in such key passages as Luke 7:22–23 and 14:13–14, 21 it is evident that Luke closely connects Jesus' own intention with what he perceives to be the church's primary mission.

The alternative lectionary selection, Acts 11:4–18, is in some ways more appropriate for public reading, since it sets forth the situation as a whole. But it also has one great disadvantage: it does not give the content of Peter's sermon. Taken alone (see 11:15), it could suggest that the connection between Jesus' ministry and the universality of the gospel is incidental, that Christianity is a kind of broad-mindedness.

In this section one should also note 11:17, a stress on God's gift which is absent from Peter's words in chapter 10 (though not from the narrative itself; see 10:45) and the dramatic way in which this emphasis allows Luke to point out that the apostles and other Judean Christians were silenced (*hesychadsō*) by what God had just showed them.

Two brief sermonic suggestions: The form of the Lukan sermon (see above) is to be highly commended. And a greater mistake could hardly be made than to imagine that the problem of our text is no longer with us. Most Christians want their churches to grow, particularly (and in some cases, only) if the new members are pretty much like the old ones. Yet the church in Korea is more pious than we are, the church in Kenya is growing faster, the church in Latin America is more committed to social justice, and the church down the street even seems to enjoy its hymns more than we do! Still in a hundred subtle (and some not very subtle) ways we thank God that we have better sense than they do.

GOSPEL: MARK 1:4–11

The "beginning" of the gospel of which Mark speaks in 1:1 is both temporal—how it all began—and foundational—what it is.

The prologue, of which our verses are a part, is increasingly held to extend from v. 1 through v. 15. This introductory section connects the public ministry of John the Baptist (1:2–11) and Jesus' preparation (baptism, 1:9–11, and temptation, 1:12–13) with the beginnings of Jesus' ministry (located in time and space, 1:14, and summarized, 1:15).

The lectionary readings which stop with v. 8 more or less independently stress John as forerunner, while the inclusion of vv. 9–11 connects the forerunner specifically with Jesus and the Spirit.

All three sections of vv. 4–15 (4–8, 9–11, 12–13) end with a solemn proclamation. Thematically, these verses affirm that (1) the Scriptures point to John, who points to Jesus, and (2) the Son, affirmed by God in the voice and the Spirit, speaks of the kingdom of God.

But who is this John who bears witness to Jesus? In Mark he is associated with the promise of Isa. 40:3 (a text also cited by the Covenanters of Qumran) and known for a ministry in the wilderness. He is dressed like Elijah, and he appears in the wilderness. He preaches "a baptism in token of repentance, for the forgiveness of sins" (NEB).

It is evident that some details of this portrait have been Christianized. The historical John probably thought of himself as the precursor of God's coming (rather than of the coming of Jesus), and his message surely included much more about judgment and much less about the Holy Spirit than our text indicates. The confession of sins (plural) at baptism sounds very much like early Christian practice.

But none of this is determinative for the question of John's significance. What is important is to note that, as with any historical figure, *significance* is an extremely complex word. And historically, neither his clothing nor his baptism nor his charism nor his message nor his following nor his death is responsible for his central place in a thousand pulpits this Sunday in Epiphany. That place is due to his association with Jesus.

Preachers with a sense of humor might note that he is by no means the last preacher of damnation and judgment whose message has been transformed by a loving God to become good news to those who come after.

The ascetic description of John's life style (v. 6; cf. Matt. 11:18 = Luke 7:33, Q) also raises an interesting question for the contemporary preacher: When does a serious call to a change of life style become fanaticism or simple folly? A despising of the world like that implied at Corinth and evident behind 1 Tim. 4:1–4 is rejected in the Scripture itself. But are most of us really in danger of ascetic zeal?

Jesus' preparation is concluded with the baptism (vv. 9–11) and the temptation (vv. 12–13). The description of the baptismal scene as an "interpretive vision" (Lentzen-Deis) is a good one; it portrays Jesus' fundamental significance as the Son of God.

V. 9 locates Jesus' call in time and space, though "immediately" in v. 10 emphasizes the presence of God, not chronology. (This term usually means something like the Semitic "And lo!")

The opening of the heavens (at the baptism) is a very widespread apocalyptic motif; it makes available to human vision what is otherwise hidden: see Ezek. 1:1; Rev. 4:1; cf. also Isa. 64:1; 3 Macc. 6:18. Mark 15:38 implies something similar. Here, as in Acts 10:4, it allows for complete access between heaven and earth.

V. 11 is a citation from Isa. 42:1. As in 9:7 (but unlike Matt. 3:17) it is the one who sees into heaven to whom the voice is addressed. The Spirit is understood as equipping for messianic office (as in the OT passage). Our verses also contain some echoes from the Isaac story in Genesis 22. The Adam parallel, however, which is clear in vv. 12–13, is not suggested in the account of the baptism.

The Markan use of these texts gives some hints about the perennial question of the use of Scripture. In some way we must find a legitimate lens beyond the severely historical one for the "eyes of faith." A tradition in some Christian circles, for example, has it that in the life to come every body will be perfect and without blemish—except the body of Jesus. Will those scars be a sign that he has "no beauty that we should desire him" (Isa. 53:2), or will they reflect a kind of beauty that Second Isaiah did not yet envision?

The Second Sunday After the Epiphany

Lutheran	Roman Catholic	Episcopal	Pres/UCC/Chr	Meth/COCU
1 Sam. 3:1–10	1 Sam. 3:3b–10, 19	1 Sam. 3:1–10, (11–20)	1 Sam. 3:1–10	1 Sam. 3:1–20
1 Cor. 6:12–20	1 Cor. 6:13c–15a, 17–20	1 Cor. 6:11b–20	1 Cor. 6:12–20	1 Cor. 6:11b–20
John 1:43–51	John 1:35–42	John 1:43–51	John 1:35–42	John 1:35–51

FIRST LESSON: 1 SAMUEL 3:1–10

1 Samuel begins with the birth of Samuel to Elkanah and Hannah; it ends with the death of Saul, king by virtue of his anointing by Samuel. Chapter 3 is concerned with the calling of Samuel, whose birth (1 Sam. 2:1–10; cf. Luke 1:46–55) and youth (2:26; cf. Luke 2:52) offer instructive parallels to the career of Jesus. The overall theme of our readings is calling and witness. (Of the three great themes of the books of Samuel—kingship, Jerusalem, and priesthood—it is the third that is central in our text.)

Samuel is called as a youth (3:1), which apparently means not so much "boy" as "one without experience or training," as in Jer. 1:6. But our ancient authors already knew how difficult it is to specify the precise qualifications for dealing with *the word of the Lord* or a *vision* from God (v. 3), so all these terms are used to show that the emphasis lies on the activity of God, not the qualities of the prophet.

It should also be noted that Samuel was called in a time when significant manifestations of God were rare (3:1); not all ages are great ages of faith. In the fifties almost everything seemed to work; in the eighties almost nothing does. But it was wrong then, and it is wrong now, to ascribe success or failure entirely to individual witnesses. *Calling* implies *God* before it implies *talent*.

Samuel's call comes to him as he sleeps in the shrine (v. 3). Isaiah's came at worship (Isa. 6:1), Jacob's at a holy "place" (Gen. 28:11, 16f.), Paul's on a road near Damascus (Gal. 1:12, 17). No pattern is normative. One might also note that while Samuel understands his calling through the mediation of Levi, the old priest is by no means an ideal figure.

V. 7 sets forth a striking parallel: "Samuel did not yet know the Lord" and "the word of the Lord had not yet been revealed to him." A crusty seminary dean of my acquaintance once received a four-page description of the kind of man (of course) desired by a particular pulpit committee. His reply was brief: "You don't say whether or not the young man should believe in God. Do you care?" In our text "knowing" the Lord means having something to say that God wants said. Everything else is mechanics.

So God comes and stands there (v. 10; RSV: "stood forth"). No absent God can call witnesses. But equally, no faithful witnesses will forever find God absent.

The message actually given to Samuel (vv. 11–14) sets many modern ears tingling; it is filled with judgment. Today we know that the negative is not God's only word, certainly not the final word. We rightly insist that judgment is the wrong word for a child dying in pain, a man struggling with alcohol, a single parent who has just been laid off. But in a world where children are tortured and the innocent are being killed (often by weapons produced in America) we cannot deny all words of judgment without denying the very character of God.

SECOND LESSON: 1 CORINTHIANS 6:11b(12)–20

It is not immediately clear why this section on food and sexual immorality should have been sandwiched between the call of Samuel and the calling of the first Christian disciples. But the selection is a good one. Paul writes to people who know themselves to be "called" by God and who therefore insist that the world's standards are no final court of appeal. Paul agrees (1 Cor. 6:4). But he denies that for those who are called the world is irrelevant or the body insignificant and reminds the Corinthians what (better: whose) they are.

First (v. 11), Paul recognizes that Christianity effects (and expects) a moral transformation. The list of vices, to be sure, emphasizes, more than most of us would, sexual matters. As Billy Graham has reminded us, two of the Ten Commandments deal with economics, only one with sex! How many sermons do we hear (from pulpit or TV set) on idolatry or greed (5:10), to say nothing of reviling (slander) or swindling (RSV: "robbers")?

So Paul demands a real transformation from real sins, and he describes this transformation in theological terms: washing (baptism), sanctification, and justification.

V. 12 at least partially explains why he prefers theological to moral categories: the Corinthian church misunderstands the work of the Spirit. If, with most commentators, we take "all things are lawful for me" as a slogan, Paul apparently accepts it, even as he asks, "But what do you mean by 'me'?" "I am a free individual" is Greek; "I am bought with a price to serve God in the body" is Christian.

The Corinthians apparently understood Christian freedom to allow either immorality or sexual asceticism (chapters 6–7) and to permit even participation in pagan meals (chapters 8–10) on the principle that all true freedom is inward. For Paul, however, "all things are yours" is just the other side of the coin on which is written, "you are Christ's" (3:21ff.).

Hence food—a thing—is free to be used. But though both food and the stomach are things and thus transient, the body itself is destined for resurrection as an aspect of the person.

Similarly sex does not involve merely things; it involves persons. So Paul eliminates two recurring misconceptions: (1) a person is defined by his or her sexuality (Freud's famous "anatomy is destiny"), and (2) sex is an act, not a relationship. He opposes both the deification and the depersonalization of sex.

The shunning of immorality (v. 18), therefore, is simply an acting out of the genuine nature of human relationships as opposed to false views, whether secular or (as in Corinth) religious.

The body could hardly be more exalted than in this whole discussion since, in our Christian freedom, its proper use is said to be to glorify God.

What is specific in 1 Samuel and John 1 is here generalized to include all Christians: we have been called by God to responsible, that is, concrete witness.

GOSPEL: JOHN 1:35(43)–51

If we begin the third reading with v. 35 (as in some lectionaries), our passage again (see the previous lesson) places John the Baptist at the beginning of Jesus' ministry. In the Gospel of John, even more clearly than in the synoptic tradition, John is portrayed as the witness par excellence to Jesus.

It is evident that our text has been carefully structured, and the links are clear:

1:35–39 John the Baptist's witness to his disciple, Andrew

1:40–42 Andrew's witness to his brother, Simon Peter

1:43–44 Jesus' (?) call to Philip (from Bethsaida, the town of Andrew and Peter)

1:45–46 Philip's witness to Nathanael

1:47–51 Jesus' call to Nathanael.

The passage is concerned with the themes of calling and witness and includes the notes of finding (vv. 41, 43, 45), coming (vv. 39, 46, 47), and following (vv. 37, 38, 40, 43).

Two themes predominate in vv. 35–42: discipleship and Christology. The section begins with Andrew and an unnamed disciple. They are pointed to Jesus by John the Baptist himself (v. 36f.), and they "follow" him. Andrew then, as a model of discipleship, brings another to Jesus—his brother, Simon Peter.

Discipleship in the Fourth Gospel, however, is by no means abstract. It is specifically related to the person of Jesus. The point is made clearly already in v. 38, where the question, "What are you looking for?" becomes, in some texts, "Whom . . . ?" Though the reading is probably secondary, the theology is thoroughly Johannine: We bring our questions to the text, and the text tells us that, when the questions are properly formulated, the answer is simply Jesus Christ. One artist has rightly caught the irony of Pilate's famous "What is truth?" (18:38) by portraying Jesus, bound before Pilate, seated high on a dais—the picture is entitled something like "The Judgment of Pilate." Had he read John 14:6 (as we have), Pilate would have formulated the question correctly and avoided the Judge he unknowingly faced.

Even the "whom" of the question, however, is difficult. Some see in our text a growing understanding on the part of the disciples, but their lack of understanding really serves only to highlight the exalted terms they use. All of the christological titles in this section have elaborate histories, some of which are discussed in most commentaries. The preacher should be cautious, however, about elaborating them from the rest of the NT without some explanation of the differences. The "Lamb" of vv. 29, 36, for example, is a purely sacrificial image; it is not identical with the Lamb-motif in Revelation, which includes not only expiation, as here (see Rev. 5:6, 12; 7:14; 12:11; 13:8), but also, among other things, the astonishing metaphor, "the Wrath of the Lamb" (see Rev. 6:16; cf. 14:10; 17:14). Similarly, in John "the Son of man," more than in the synoptics, has overtones of glorification.

A final note on christological terms: It is possible, though a bit strained, to understand v. 45, "the one of whom Moses in the law and also the prophets wrote," as a reference to the "prophet like Moses" of Deut. 18:15, 18 and the Elijah of Mal. 4:5. If this were correct (and it may not be), then our text would ascribe to Jesus precisely the three titles John refuses for himself in v. 25.

Clearly, though early Christianity had no uniform way of understanding either the Scripture or John the Baptist, both pointed to Jesus. So in John it is Andrew (not Peter) who first acknowledges Jesus as the Messiah (v. 41; cf. Mark 8:29). But in both John and the synoptic traditions the designation is considered appropriate. And here, as in Matthew, Peter's confession results in his being given a new name. (On this motif, see Gen. 17:4; 32:28.)

Two characters from our text suggest themselves as sermonic possibilities, Philip and Andrew. In John alone is significant narrative material connected with Philip; see 6:5ff.; 12:21f.; 14:8f. He somehow cannot seem to get things right, either when questioned about feeding the multitudes (6:5) or when trying to understand the relationships between the Father and the Son (14:8). But he knows that Jesus is Lord (14:8), and he is a faithful witness for both Nathanael (1:45f.) and some unnamed Greeks (12:21f.).

The material on Andrew is also somewhat limited. (Bethsaida was predominantly Gentile, so he has a Greek name.) But he too is a faithful witness, to his own brother (1:41), to the Greeks (12:21f.), and possibly (the Greek is not clear) to Philip, his fellow townsman (1:43).

The final figure of importance in our text is Nathanael, mentioned only in John. He is a believing Israelite, known by Jesus even as he sits quietly under a fig tree. (Because of the rabbinic tradition that the fig tree was associated with learning, Augustine suggests that Nathanael was too learned to be one of the Twelve!) His name is common in many languages: "God has given" is the thought behind such names as Nathan, Jonathan, Adeodatus (Augustine's son), Theodore and Theodora, and that peculiarly pious American name, Increase (see 1 Cor. 3:6 KJV).

Nathanael's question, "Can anything good come from Nazareth?" is instructive. We too easily dismiss as simple prejudice attitudes that begin by being ethnic. One who does not understand the power of nationalism (which is merely local pride on a much larger scale) cannot understand most of the serious problems of the twentieth century. Nathanael is not a bad man; he is just unprepared for God's wider vision. That he is "without guile"—a term familiar to readers of the OT (Gen. 27:35; Isa. 53:9)—means that for John a Jew *qua* Jew is not hypocritical.

The promise, "You will see greater things," (v. 50) looks ahead to the miracle at Cana (2:1–11) and also to all that follows. Luther's statement, "Conversion is the greatest of all miracles," is a just commentary on 5:21.

Finally, we might ask why the notion of a bridge between heaven and earth (the Jacob metaphor in v. 51) resonates so inadequately today. Is the problem merely astronomical? Or could it also be that we have so deified humanity and domesticated God that neither we nor our congregations are conscious of any gap that needs to be bridged?

The Third Sunday After the Epiphany

Lutheran	Roman Catholic	Episcopal	Pres/UCC/Chr	Meth/COCU
Jon. 3:1–5, 10	Jon. 3:1–5, 10	Jer. 3:21—4:2	Jon. 3:1–5, 10	Jon. 3:1–5, 10
1 Cor. 7:29–31	1 Cor. 7:29–31	1 Cor. 7:17–23	1 Cor. 7:29–31	1 Cor. 7:29–35
Mark 1:14–20	Mark 1:14–20	Mark 1:14–20	Mark 1:14–20	Mark 1:14–20

FIRST LESSON: JONAH 3:1–5, 10

The book of Jonah consists of a prayer—possibly quite ancient though inserted into this postexilic book (2:2–9)—and three incidents: Jonah and the ship (chap. 1), Jonah in Nineveh (chap. 3), and Jonah and the (castor oil?) plant (chap. 4). The fish incident (1:17; 2:1, 10) is told in very brief compass, and the words of Jonah himself are remarkably few (1:9, 12; 3:4b; 4:2–3, 8c). In other words, the book is mostly dramatic narrative.

The incident in today's reading is the second: Jonah in Nineveh. The word of the Lord comes to Jonah "the second time" (3:1), the first not having turned out so well. God had called Jonah to go east, so he went west. He took a ship to run away from the call of God, and, as the author naively reminds us, "he paid the fare thereof" (1:3 KJV). (This phrase is only one of several striking sermon texts in this brief book; see also 1:10, 14; 2:9, 10; 3:5, 6, 9, 10; 4:4, 11.)

But the word did not get lost just because Jonah did. The word remains sure; Jonah waivers. (Cf. Jer. 15:19.)

Yet it comes now to a different Jonah, "resurrected" from the fish. (Cf. Matt. 12:40.) Like Tarwater in Flannery O'Connor's remarkable *The Violent Bear It Away,* he does not like the word he is given, but he faithfully passes it on. Incidentally, it is summarized as one of the shortest sermons in the Bible, only about half a dozen words.

It should be noted that the common view of Jonah as a kind of particularist bigot is not necessarily correct. He does not really want the sailors to die. He finds no satisfaction either in delivering his message of judgment (though it brings a whole city to repentance) or in God's staying of judgment. After Nineveh repents, Jonah confesses that God is "slow to anger and abounding in steadfast love" (4:2)— but that is exactly the view that impelled him toward Tarshish in the first place. Jonah really just wants to die.

Why? The text is not completely clear. It suggests only that he had a perfectly sound view of God (4:2) but just was not very enthusiastic about carrying out the challenging task that view implied. This is still true, and it is a better sermonic possibility than stressing the "particularist/universalist" contrast in such a way as to portray Christians as broadminded and tolerant, Jews as bigoted and provincial. (A stronger, if not completely conclusive, case could be made for the reverse!)

By our author's time, Nineveh has become a mere symbol. Ancient records indicate its greatness, but its destruction (612 B.C.) came long before the writing of this book. It is easy to smile at those who would claim some great city for Christ in our day; but Jonah is perhaps closer to them than to those who think only in lesser, more gradualist and "realistic" terms.

The forty days (v. 4; in some texts, "three days more") is a symbolic number, common in the Bible. Here it suggests immediacy. (It is rare, though not unknown, for prophets to include specific chronologies; see Isa. 7:16; 8:4; 16:14; 23:15–17; Jer. 25:11–12; 28:16; 29:10—all of which involve much longer periods of time.)

To "believe" God (v. 5) seems to involve several elements: to accept the truth preached; to repent, that is, to turn from evil; to "cry mightily to God," presumably for rescue; and to hope for salvation from judgment (vv. 5–9). Here salvation is both universal and corporate. Note the concatenation of texts: "And the people . . . believed God" (v. 5) while "the king . . . removed his robe" (v. 6). Before God there are no kings—only people. In the context, the authorities, the people, and even the animals are bound in a common fate.

It might be noted that the only specific sin mentioned, in v. 8, is violence.

The inconsistency of Jonah's God is in complete conformity with Jeremiah's view (Jer. 18:5–10) and the Hebrew prophetic tradition as a whole. The speculative question, whether God can change his mind, is not very important. The faithfulness of God is.

SECOND LESSON: 1 CORINTHIANS 7:29–31 (35)

Chapter 7 as a whole is Paul's response to certain questions addressed to him in a letter from the Corinthian church (7:1). Our section (vv. 29–35) is the second of three having to do with virginity: vv. 25–28 suggest that in the light of the eschatological situation, it is equally acceptable to be married or unmarried—though the former group will have more trouble (vv. 28, 40); vv. 29–35 give the famous *hōs . . . me* (as if . . . not) an application to the married life (and other circumstances); vv. 36–38 deal with the special question of giving one's daughter (or accepting one's affianced) in marriage.

It is striking that Paul, in giving such concrete advice on a particular problem, draws his conclusions from his theological outlook as a whole, based on reality as he understands it.

The critical principle, here given many-sided force, is that neither the world nor any aspect of concrete existence can be finally determinative for the Christian. To be married, to weep and rejoice, to buy, to "make use of the world"—these are simply the givens within which the Christian life must be lived. But this is not the last word. The world is passing away. And then: God.

Vv. 32–35 show why, in Paul's view, the implication of the "as if

. . . not" points toward the single, that is, unencumbered life. Probably if he were pushed (and today we would all like to push him just a little!) he would admit the other side of the coin as well—that the single life can also be full of encumbrances, while the married state often brings both husband and wife to more single-minded Christian lives.

But the principle remains the same: (1) the Christian lives in the world, makes decisions in the world, serves God and others in the world, lives and proclaims the Word of God in the world; and (2) the world is passing away.

Obviously, if Paul had drawn the conclusion that the world is therefore either objectionable or irrelevant, if he had spiritualized the Christian life, he would have had no problems in Corinth. That he did have problems shows how complex his thought is. Otherworldliness is not Pauline—but neither are most forms of secular theology. The last word comes not from the *saeculum*—its culture, its morals, its economic and nationalistic aspirations—it comes from God.

Some preachers will be more comfortable than others with the apocalyptic and eschatological imagery of vv. 26, 29, 31. But we all need to ponder deeply the *intellectual* error implicit in Philo's comment, "We know that the human race will endure forever." That is precisely what we do not know. We must deal instead with John Donne's question, "What if this present were the world's last night?" Then it becomes irrelevant whether God's instrument in bringing history to a close will be human folly or some unexpected earthly or astronomical phenomenon. It will end. And that is Paul's point.

The easiest way to transform prophetic witness into ideology, in other words, is to forget the "as if . . . not."

GOSPEL: MARK 1:14–20

Like Matthew (4:17), Mark gives a summary of Jesus' teaching (1:14–15). This summary is followed in our reading by the calling of the first four disciples: Simon and Andrew, James and John.

The association of these two sections in all our lectionaries hints at a very significant point: following Jesus has a particular content. It is no mere feeling, no romanticized inclination toward a compelling figure, no self-evident turning from a wicked (or boring) world to a man from Nazareth whose person and message we can create for ourselves.

It is generally recognized that the content—though not the precise wording—of 1:14–15 is faithful to the teaching of Jesus a generation earlier. Jesus is located in time and space (v. 14; cf. v. 9), and his teaching is summarized in a twofold form of a single statement ("the time is fulfilled, and the kingdom [reign] of God is at hand"), followed by a twofold form of a single imperative ("repent, and believe in the gospel").

That Jesus came (v. 14) shows, like Mark as a whole, the importance of Jesus as model; but that he came *preaching* shows that the prophetic vocation demands more than an attractive life style. For Mark, who Jesus was and what he said cannot be separated. The burden of Jesus' public preaching, the "gospel of God," is given in Christian terminology; see Rom. 1:1; 15:16; 1 Cor. 11:7; 1 Thess. 2:2, 8; 1 Pet. 4:17. But Jesus may well have been familiar with the use of the verb *bśr* (Greek: *euaggelidsomai*), to bring good news, which occurs in second Isaiah (52:7; 61:1).

The notion of the fulfillment of time is apocalyptic, but Jesus, unlike apocalyptic writers, rarely gives evidence drawn from the historical realm. (Mark 13, which gives signs of the end of the age, includes a good deal of material that originated after the resurrection, and it omits any emphasis on the fulfillment already present in Jesus' ministry.) The reason for this difference is apparently that Jesus' conviction rests on the promise and activity of God, not on current events. This is not a de-historicizing of the Good News. It is rather a solemn awareness that God reveals the meaning of history, not the other way around.

That God's reign (a better translation than kingdom or realm, since it is more personal and less spatial) has drawn near is a symbol of God's action: a dynamic, not a static, understanding of God's ways in the world. It implies, especially coupled with a call for repentance and faith, a stress on God's will to save. Repentance is thus primarily a way to participate in the saving activity of God, only secondarily to escape from the wrath to come; in Jesus' teaching it means turning toward a God who has already turned toward us. In classical terminology Jesus differs from prophecy, apocalyptic, and John the Baptist in that he conceives of salvation as God's proper work, judgment as God's strange work *(opus proprium/opus alienum)*.

What shall we preach? John preached repentance (1:4); Jesus preached the Gospel of God (1:14); the church preaches "the gospel" (of Jesus Christ) (1:1; 8:35; 10:29; 13:10; 14:9). Each stage requires the earlier one(s) as foundation, the later one(s) as content and verification.

"Calling" scenes in the Bible like those in vv. 16–20 typically have three parts: (1) the situation, (2) the call, and (3) the response. (See 2:13–14; 10:17–22; John 1:35–42; and cf. 1 Kings 19:19–21 [Elisha]; Acts 26:12–20 [Paul].) The "response" usually involves both negative and positive acts, renunciation and witness. Both aspects are important: The former without the latter leads to asceticism and other-worldliness; the latter without the former is not credible.

Notice that Jesus does not engage in any symbolic act; cf. 1 Kings 19:19 and the words of the hymn, "Elijah's mantle o'er Elisha cast." He simply calls. The fourth-century philosopher Porphyry suggested that the disciples came immediately (vv. 18, 20) and unquestioningly because they were not very intelligent. But when Jesus calls, as Mark makes clear, we are faced with a decision about the importance of Jesus, not about our IQ.

"Fishers"—an old English word now being brought back into use in a gesture toward sexually inclusive language—suggests that the church's message is aimed at people rather than at abstractions or causes.

These two incidents are for Mark pointers to the twin themes of mission and discipleship. Two elements in them are of particular importance.

The first is that these disciples are called individually, like Paul, not in throngs, as at Pentecost or (often) in the history of missions or indigenous churches. Christianity became a mass movement; it did not start out that way.

The second important element in the Markan understanding of calling is that the disciples' mission involves suffering and service. In Mark—unlike Luke-Acts, where a different point is emphasized—Christian theology is seen as a *theologia crucis,* and discipleship is understood in terms of suffering service, proclaimed and modeled by Jesus as the good news of salvation.

The Fourth Sunday After the Epiphany

Lutheran	Roman Catholic	Episcopal	Pres/UCC/Chr	Meth/COCU
Deut. 18:15-20	Deut. 18:15-20	Deut. 18:15-20	Deut. 18:15-22	Deut. 18:15-22
1 Cor. 8:1-13	1 Cor. 7:32-35	1 Cor. 8:1b-13	1 Cor. 7:32-35	1 Cor. 8:1-13
Mark 1:21-28	Mark 1:21-28	Mark 1:21-28	Mark 1:21-28	Mark 1:21-28

FIRST LESSON: DEUTERONOMY 18:15-20(22)

Our text occurs in the long central section of Deuteronomy (4:44—26:19) that includes Moses' exposition of the law. The exposition is preceded by a hortatory speech (4:44—11:32) and followed by the formulation of a covenant (26:16–19).

The few verses in the lectionary, 18:15–22, are themselves part of a discussion of prophecy, in which a very sharp distinction is made between prophecy in Israel and a variety of mantic and magical practices known in the surrounding cultures. Essentially two points are made: (1) Prophecy cannot include ordeal by fire, divination, magic, or any attempt to communicate with, or gain power over, supernatural forces. (The precise meaning of the terms in vv. 10–11 is occasionally obscure, but the force of the prohibition is clear.) God is not at the disposal of any human or supernatural power; he communicates his will. (The principle still applies; if you try to call the president of the United States, you will almost certainly fail; if he tries to call you, he will almost certainly succeed.) (2) Even those who purport to bring a message from God may not be doing so: the word spoken may not be from God, or the prophet may be speaking in the name of false gods (v. 20), these offenses to be punished by death; or the word itself may be untrue (Heb.: "the word is not," possibly equals *the word does not happen;* so the LXX) or is not fulfilled (vv. 21–22).

The presupposition of our text, therefore, is that God will continue to guide the people in the meaning and application of the law (the two are less separable in Deuteronomy than they are for us), but that guidance is to be obtained only from those who rightly set forth the Word of God.

The prophet par excellence for our text is Moses, who was allowed to mediate between the people and God because of the people's fear (5:23–27). But he will be followed by others who, like him, are to be listened to (vv. 15, 19, 22).

The original reference of our verses is doubtless plural, to those prophets (cf. the collective use of "king" in 17:14–15) who in subsequent years should declare the Word of God.

But Judaism, unlike some contemporary historicist scholars, was never content with the original reference. The Essenes at Qumran (1 Q S 9:1; 4 Q Testimonia), the Samaritans, and possibly even the Pharisees (see John 1:21, 24, 25) seem to have envisioned a specific figure who would declare the Word of God at the end of time.

Early Christianity understood Jesus in precisely this way; see Acts 3:22–23; 7:37, where the text is understood to foretell not only Jesus as prophet but his resurrection as well (Heb.: "raise up"; LXX: *anastēsei*). As both prophet and risen Lord, he continues to speak in the name of God, who has put His words into Jesus' mouth (Deut. 18:18–19; cf. John 12:49–50).

Once more our text reflects both the dilemma and the opportunity of the modern preacher. Not only Judaism and the Christian church, but the people of God from the earliest times reflected in our text are concerned to hear the Word of God anew. The NT writers do not handle the OT text like modern seminarians; neither do the rabbis. And neither does the OT itself. Deuteronomy is a second hearing of the law, a promise that God's will can still be known—because God is making it known.

Some careful safeguards against presumption are included in the text, and they (and others) must always be observed when any preacher, teacher, parent, or neighbor presumes to know the divine will for the life of an individual or a community. But the promise that God will continually make his word known justifies the risk of trying to hear it and, in every age, to proclaim it anew.

SECOND LESSON: 1 CORINTHIANS 8:1–13

It is clear that 1 Corinthians is made up in large part of certain matters about which Paul knew the Corinthians to have had difficulty, either on the basis of a letter to him (7:1) or because of what he had heard from Chloe's people (1:11) or others. One such matter concerned the eating of food sacrificed to idols (8:1), that is, food which in a variety of ways had been associated with pagan worship, either before being placed on the market or in the course of a social or public event in a temple or a home. Food not included in this category was generally available, though as one writer has whimsically but not unjustly observed, the ordinary Attic diet consisted of two courses, the first a kind of porridge, and the second a kind of porridge!

Yet meat was occasionally eaten, and what was available often had been tainted in some way by contact with idolatrous religious practices. In this situation the Corinthians—as they often did—thought in slogans. (Cf. the JB translation of 1:12: "all these slogans that you have.") It is true, and Paul largely agrees, that "we all have knowledge" (8:1), that "idols do not really exist in the world" (8:4), that "we suffer no disadvantage if we do not eat, nor any advantage if we do" (8:8), and so on. Against any legalism that is indifferent to people and consequences for the sake of the rule itself, Paul and his opponents both rightly insist on the Christian's liberty to do the will of God.

But there is more than one way of forgetting God in one's religious zeal. And the Corinthians were apparently determined to hold to their rights as Christian freedmen, heedless of all consequences. In so doing, they absolutized their slogans into immutable—and ahistorical—principles, substituting a rule for responsible action.

This, says Paul, will not do. Meat itself is unimportant and will never bring us to God, for either judgment or grace (8:8). The "strong" know this. But others, "weak" because they have been habituated to the religious significance of food sacrificed to idols (8:7), cannot eat such food without violating their Christian consciences. For the sake of such people and the mortal danger into which I will put them by insisting on my rights (vv. 11–13), I will simply abstain from meat.

Two practical comments are appropriate here. For one thing, Paul is simply indifferent to the ordinary Jewish regulations about meat: Has it come into contact with idolaters? Has it been correctly slaughtered? Is it forbidden in the law? The perfectly correct impulse in our day toward insisting on Paul's essential Jewishness has to some degree overlooked this fundamental point.

Again, it should be noted that Paul and his opponents really differ not simply about meat but about the meaning of freedom. For the Corinthians "knowledge" set the individual above history, beyond the realm of concrete decisions in an ambiguous world, beyond the needs of other believers, and thus beyond the concrete demands of the living God. For Paul "knowledge" is subsumed under love, and my neighbor's concrete good has priority over my rights. Paul (fortunately) never suggests that a good argument with a weak brother might not be a salutary thing. But he knows that the God who is our source and goal (8:6) and Jesus Christ, who created and redeemed us (8:6, 11), are more interested in my Christian sisters and brothers than in my principles. Even a mistaken Christian is still one for whom Christ died, so I must not interpose my principles between a fellow believer and that saving death. Perhaps nowhere in all of ancient literature is there a clearer statement of human rights, including the right to be wrong with impunity.

The larger theological issue is not, ultimately, unlike that posed in Deut. 18:15–20: Is the law of God an abstraction, or does it have to be rethought and restated (not rejected!) as new situations arise? Only congregations that side with the Deuteronomist and Paul on this critical matter will ever really be open to a new hearing of the eternal Word. And only prophets/preachers who are fully aware of its risk will stand any real chance of proclaiming it.

GOSPEL: MARK 1:21–28

Today's reading (vv. 21–28) is part of a longer section in which Jesus, having called the first four disciples (vv. 16–20), enters Capernaum (v. 21) and on the Sabbath teaches and heals in the synagogue (vv. 21b–28); heals Simon Peter's mother-in-law (vv. 29–31); and then performs many other miracles of healing and exorcism (vv. 32–34).

In our verses the emphasis is on Jesus' authority, evident in his teaching and his power over the demons, a "new teaching" (vv. 22, 27; cf. also v. 21). Far more than the other evangelists, Mark portrays Jesus as a teacher.

To be sure, the "immediately" of v. 21 is more dramatic than chronological; its effect is to connect it with v. 22 and thus to heighten the impression of Jesus' authority.

In v. 22 "astonished" is a very strong word. (Cf. 6:2; 10:26; 11:18.) It indicates that Jesus far exceeds the crowd's expectations.

It should be noted that his learning is not what distinguishes Jesus from the scribes. True, the Markan Jesus recognizes cleverness when he meets it (7:29), he bests his opponents in argument (12:13–37), he instructs a scribe in the essence of the Law (12:28–34), he attacks Temple practices in his teaching (11:15–18), and so on. But everywhere the emphasis is on the authority with which he speaks.

The modern preacher could do much worse than to pause and reflect on this fact. There is nothing wrong with being learned, clever, witty, rhetorically skilled, discerning—the list is endless—in one's preaching. Furthermore, the reverse—ignorant, pedestrian, dull, monotonous, insensitive—is certainly even worse. Yet technique is no substitute for powerful substance. Swinburne once noted of W. E. Henley that it was tragic for such great powers of expression to have been given to someone with so little to express. Empty rhetoric may be popular, and it won't get you killed. But it is not Christian preaching. To say something and to say it with authority is still an art.

As the controversy in 2:1–12 shows, the scribes' problem is not that they do not know the Scripture. It is rather, from Mark's viewpoint, that they misunderstand who Jesus is.

The exorcism itself is told in typical form: (1) the encounter with Jesus, including the use of name and data (the terms reflect 1 Kings 17:18) in a futile attempt to gain control over Jesus (v. 24), (2) the exorcism proper, including the silencing (literally, muzzling) with a mere word (v. 25), (3) the evidence for the miracle (the convulsing of the man, the demon's loud cry, v. 26), and (4) the reaction of the crowd (v. 27) and the resulting spread of Jesus' fame (v. 28). One unusual feature is the sudden intrusion of the plural, "us," in v. 24, a literary way of pointing out that Jesus is a threat to the whole demonic world.

In this instance, no objection is raised to the working of the miracle on the Sabbath, a discussion which Mark postpones for a more convenient season (3:1–6).

The conceptuality here is not specifically Christian. Most Jews and Gentiles at the beginning of our era shared with Christians the view that demonic forces not only possessed an unfortunate few individuals but also were lying in wait for others. Self-exorcism is almost unknown, so without a powerful healer anyone in danger of possession was threatened with a total loss of human freedom.

Only in this context—that Jesus Christ frees one completely from the threat of such loss—is the widespread understanding of Christianity as a liberating force in the ancient world fully comprehensible. Because today we tend to think of our human freedoms as endangered only by other individuals, we lack this profound sense.

Similarly, Jesus' exorcisms are seen in the earliest traditions (probably including Jesus' own lifetime) as signs of the inbreaking kingdom of God (Matt. 12:28 = Luke 11:20), as tokens of the liberating effect of Jesus' ministry among humanity. We are set free, this symbol suggests, both from and for the world.

Note that Jesus' "new teaching" (v. 27) is not new in content. In the ancient world the old rather than the new is generally considered to be true. Jesus' teaching (which for Mark includes his actions) is new in its power.

It is not insignificant that the healed man completely disappears from the text. Mark is not primarily concerned for him. He is concerned rather to show who Jesus is. In v. 27, to be sure, the question is "What," not "Who?" But, as the verbal parallels with 4:41 shows, the question is not really a different one. What it conveys is, Who is this one who teaches and acts in this powerful new way?

The Fifth Sunday After the Epiphany

Lutheran	Roman Catholic	Episcopal	Pres/UCC/Chr	Meth/COCU
Job 7:1–7	Job. 7:1–4, 6–7	2 Kings 4:(8–17) 18–21 (22–31) 32–37	Job. 7:1–7	Job. 7:1–7
1 Cor. 9:16–23	1 Cor. 9:16–19, 22–23	1 Cor. 9:16–23	1 Cor. 9:16–19, 22–23	1 Cor. 9:16–23
Mark 1:29–39	Mark 1:29–39	Mark 1:29–39	Mark 1:29–39	Mark 1:29–39

FIRST LESSON: JOB 7:1–7

This passage is not one preachers will want to dwell on for very long. Yet the experience reflected is nearly universal.

The translation of the Hebrew is often obscure, though its general tenor is clear: Job has just asked rhetorically, "Have I lost my sense of taste? Do I not really understand the full nature of my misfortunes?" Now he begins a new lament: Life is terribly hard for him (vv. 1–6), and God has forgotten Job's precarious state (v. 7).

In v. 1 "hard service" seems to be a military word. Life is a constant engagement with pain, suffering, and death. Note that Job does not contrast his own suffering with the well-being of others. Life itself, not just his private experience, is hard.

The distinction is a terribly important one. Most of us feel our own pain far more deeply than another's. (Hence the surgeons' definition: Minor surgery is surgery on somebody else!) Most of the people within the hearing of any particular sermon are reasonably well-off—or they would not be in church. Their pain may nonetheless be real, and they should be encouraged to think of others who suffer equally, if differently. Sympathy has produced more creative justice than guilt ever will.

The "hireling" (vv. 1, 2) awaits pay for work rendered. Today, this comes at the end of the week or the month. In the ancient world, where life was chancy (and employers often less scrupulous), payment was made at the end of each day. In v. 2 the hireling is a slave, laboring in the sun, longing for the shade.

In vv. 3–4 note that Job's tragic situation is not temporary. It goes on for months, seemingly endless, worst at night when even sleep is denied him. Today it is not unusual to find hospital patients, even those in serious pain, quite cheerful following a good night's rest. The "ravell'd sleeve of care" has been knit up, the "balm of hurt minds" has done its soothing work. But God has given Job only "nights of misery." When he does lie down, he thrashes from dusk to dawn.

The description in v. 5 is not completely clear; some combination of dirt, worms, scabs, and infection seems to be implied. And this is the lot of a man "blameless and upright . . . who feared God and turned away from evil" (1:1)!

Now (v. 6) Job gives the other side of the same coin. Life, which drags on interminably, is still "swifter than a weaver's shuttle" and ends without hope (of recovery). The same Hebrew word means "hope" or "thread," and the double entendre "Lack of thread/lack of hope" is surely deliberate. Here, too, we are dealing with a common experience: "Life isn't worth living, and it will be over before I know it!"

So (v. 7) Job asks God to remember all of this. The God whom Job reproaches for being unjust is still all the hope he has. The paradox is not unlike that in John 6:68: It is not God or someone else; it is God or nothing.

But there is a difference. We know that Jesus Christ has conquered death. Job did not. (Here [vv. 7f.] the denial of the resurrection seems to be implied, though 19:24–27 could indicate some progress toward a more hopeful doctrine.)

Nowhere perhaps in today's readings is the hermeneutical question posed more clearly for the modern preacher. Do we stop with what Job says of life's pain and pointlessness? Is the OT to be taken on its own terms or interpreted in the light of the One who came not to destroy but to "fulfill" it (Matt. 5:17)? For some, the former is not Christian; for others, the latter is not intellectually respectable.

No doubt time and circumstance—as well as the theological outlook and psychological stance of the preacher—have their parts to play in deciding this issue. But the next two readings for today show how two major NT thinkers understood the question. And their response is unequivocal.

SECOND LESSON: 1 CORINTHIANS 9:16–23

This chapter is a Pauline defense of his apostleship—clearly a matter of dispute between him and his opponents. In vv. 1–2, Paul gives the critical requirements of apostleship: a vision of the risen Lord (v. 1) and a call to witness. He also refers throughout the chapter (vv. 4–14) to his right as an apostle to be supported by the people among whom he labors.

His central point, however—once that right is established—is that he will not exercise it in Corinth (v. 15) because he wants the basis of his ministry to be unequivocal: he has been commissioned (vv. 16, 17).

In a series of metaphors and contrasts, Paul now insists that (1) he would not do anything else, but (2) preaching is not a pleasure. Details include the notion that he is under *anankē,* necessity; it is, so to speak, his fate to preach. Failure to preach would make him miserable (v. 16). V. 17 argues—purely rhetorically—that if he had chosen to preach, there might be some reward in it. As it is, however, he was (like Jeremiah) given no real option.

An acquaintance of mine, under circumstances which I have long since forgotten, once had to give a list of possible long-range vocational objectives to the somewhat crusty captain of his ship. The first two items were things he had long considered; in third place, because he needed a longer list and because he really had thought a good deal about it, my friend wrote down "the ministry." "Anderson," the captain told him, "that goes down first, or it doesn't go down at all!" The principle goes far beyond the clergy; it extends to every follower of Christ. When God calls, we answer.

Paradoxically, then, Paul's "reward" is that he gets no reward. Even his refusal to be supported by the Corinthians (v. 18b) is theologically motivated: the gospel must be "free," "without expense." (Not without demand!)

Then, in perhaps the most striking metaphor in the whole section, Paul says that his "freedom" (cf. 9:1) enables him to serve as slave to all. Not slave of God only, but slave of all humankind. He works for nothing except the possibility of gaining converts. Paul is not concerned for any of the things on the vocational questionnaires: fame, money, possibilities for promotion, job satisfaction, even (except in a very limited way) benefit to society. Even such ancient commonplaces as "accommodation" (to one's audience) and "renunciation" (of the world) do not explain his life. His goal, as he promised in 2:1–5, is to make the saving power of the cross evident in his own life.

That is the reason vv. 20–22 sound at first reading almost unprincipled (a conclusion drawn already in his own lifetime; see Gal. 1:10). When he is among Jews, he observes those practices whose denial would cause offense; among Gentiles, he ignores Jewish customs that Gentiles found offensive or silly, not because he has no convictions, but because his fundamental conviction—the centrality of the gospel of the cross—is so firm. Christ is the norm of Christian conduct (9:21b), and the saving of some by the preaching of the gospel is the only way to "share in its blessings" (v. 23).

Two brief homiletical suggestions: First of all, Paul knows that life is a hard service. But he also knows that the battle of life has been not ignored but won. (At least one university computer system known to me includes the command "prettify." When these buttons are pushed, the various data will be rearranged neatly into clean, beautiful columns of figures. There is no such button for the Christian life.)

The second suggestion, if the preacher wishes to concentrate on this Pauline text, has to do with evangelism. It is sometimes argued that even an evangelistic method that produces no converts may justify itself in terms of the spiritual benefits to the congregation or group involved. This may occasionally be true. On balance, however, it is dangerous nonsense. The sharing of the gospel, Paul reminds us, has as its goal the "winning" of others (vv. 20–22), not whatever subjective benefits may issue from this attempt. A "failed" evangelistic program may indeed produce benefits for those who already acknowledge Christ as Lord. But it may also show that we have used inappropriate methods in the first place. Our broken, suffering, despairing world does not need our subjective benefits; it does need our gospel and our service.

GOSPEL: MARK 1:29–39

Mark now adds to the public healing (of vv. 23–28) a private healing, Peter's mother-in-law (1:29–31). These two incidents are then followed by two summaries, vv. 32–34 and vv. 35–39.

First, the incident of healing Simon Peter's mother-in-law: This brief miracle is the only healing of a fever in the Gospels. (In John 4:52, the fever is only a symptom, not the disease itself.) The presence of the four disciples is doubly motivated: They are witnesses to the healing and also to Jesus' ministry as a whole. It is noteworthy that someone tells Jesus of the woman's illness. The four disciples merely form a bridge between Jesus' powers and the woman's need.

If the overall theme of our three pericopes is slavery and freedom, it is important to note that Simon's mother-in-law's freedom is restored by Jesus alone. The world has one Messiah; it needs no others, either individuals or nations. And Christians are as dangerous as any other messianic pretenders when they forget that fact. We are witnesses, a bridge between human need and the saving power of God. How can anyone boast of being a bridge? The hand of Jesus (vv. 31, 41) has more power to set free than all our moral indignation or pretensions.

We learn here only indirectly (and from 1 Cor. 9:5 directly) that Peter was married. Have you ever heard a sermon on his wife?

We miss an important point if we think of Peter's mother-in-law's service (1:31b) as only more evidence for women's traditional role in the world. Why might she not serve as a model for all Christians? Set free by Jesus, she serves, not merely him, but Peter and others as well.

Second, the summary (vv. 32–34): Mark's peculiar "when evening had come, when the sun had set" may have been meant to indicate the end of the sabbath (which ends at sundown). What is important, however, is that the healings and exorcisms (in that order in both vv. 32 and 34) are now said to be common. This is surely historical bedrock, on any responsible understanding of early Christian history.

Theologically, it is a mistake to attempt to defend (or deny) the existence of the demonic per se. Just as sin is best understood in the light of saving grace, so the demonic is best explained from the standpoint of its conquest in Christ.

The "silencing" of the demons (1:34b; 3:11–12) is one aspect of the famous "messianic secret." The demons know of Jesus' nature and are refused the right to speak; the disciples learn of Jesus' nature (8:29; 9:2–8) and are also refused permission to make it known (8:30; 9:9). In Mark's theology the resurrection may not be proclaimed (9:9) or experienced (8:34–37) apart from the cross.

Third, the ministry throughout Galilee (vv. 35–39): This section is, like the preceding verses, a summary. Very early in the morning (v. 35), Jesus withdraws to a remote place to pray. The crowds ("everyone," v. 37), however, are still excited about his healings and exorcisms. When Simon and his friends find him, Jesus decides to go on around the area "preaching." He "came out," Jesus says (probably from Capernaum into the whole Galilean region, though a reference to his "coming" from God is just barely possible) to preach (1:38b; cf. 1:14, 21—Mark does not separate "preaching" and "teaching"). "Casting out demons" (1:39b) is also a part of Jesus' ministry, though it is mentioned here primarily to introduce the healing which immediately follows (1:40–45).

Today, we make perhaps two opposite errors with respect to preaching. Sometimes we understand it as almost the only thing the clergy do. (Jesus a *clergyman?*) On the other hand, occasionally we depreciate it in comparison with the other social and service activities of the church. Neither will do. Every father who tells his children about Jesus, every church league softball coach explaining to her team what Christian sportsmanship is, every agency preparing a report or a program to deal with hunger or unjustice—all are "preaching."

Yet "preaching" in its traditional sense as exposition of the Word of God is never to be swallowed up by the larger conception. What we believe is at least as important as how we show what believing is.

The Sixth Sunday After the Epiphany

Lutheran	Roman Catholic	Episcopal	Pres/UCC/Chr	Meth/COCU
2 Kings 5:1–14	Lev. 13:1–2, 44–46	2 Kings 5:1–15b	Lev. 13:1–2, 44–46	2 Kings 5:1–15b, or Lev. 13:1–2, 44–46
1 Cor. 9:24–27	1 Cor. 10:31— 11:1	1 Cor. 9:24–27	1 Cor. 10:31— 11:1	1 Cor. 9:24–27; 10:31—11:1
Mark 1:40–45	Mark 1:40–45	Mark 1:40–45	Mark 1:40–45	Mark 1:40–45

FIRST LESSON: 2 KINGS 5:1–15b

Two of the three texts for this Sunday involve leprosy; the other draws its metaphors from the world of athletics. These apparently disparate narratives have several themes in common, however, of which the greatest is probably the majesty and power of the one we serve.

In the Elisha story, we meet a single prophet (cf. 2 Kings 4:1, 38; 6:1) encountering a military commander, Naaman the Syrian, who is a leper. The narrative contrasts the power of God with even the greatest earthly kings and produces (v. 15b) a remarkable monotheistic confession.

V. 1 sets forth the necessary details: Naaman is a great man, in favor with both the king of Syria and the God of Israel, who has given him military victory. But he is a leper. (The term used is a broad one and includes a variety of skin ailments besides Hansen's disease.) The case is not, apparently, serious enough to require a total quarantine (cf. Lev. 13:45–46), at least according to Syrian custom. Yet v. 7 makes it clear that the disease was incurable.

As often in the Scripture, a very minor character precipitates the action. A nameless "maid" boasts about a prophet from her homeland. What if she had been reticent about her religion?

One of the glories of narrative, especially for preaching, is the way it brings flesh-and-blood human beings onto center stage. Clearly no speculation about the age or qualities of the girl is verifiable or even historically meaningful. But the hearers of this story inevitably do create fantasies of their own as it is told, involving themselves in the action, visualizing the people and the scene, and so on. Are there no pious little girls in our congregations who might be delighted to dream, not about the loathsomeness of the disease (yuck!) but about the importance of sharing their love for the people of God? Or men and women of power and authority who know how often they are asked to play God—to provide jobs in a failing economy, to redirect national and international policies that they often could not change even if they knew how? (Henry Kissinger once said that the difficulty of making fundamental changes in American foreign policy reminded him of the Australian who needed a new boomerang but couldn't get one because he couldn't throw his old one away!) There is something of each one of us in the characters of this dramatic tale. (So sin boldly—exploit the narrative!)

The action is fairly straightforward. Naaman tells the king of the girl's word, the Syrian king sends gifts to the king of Israel, the king of Israel is terrified, and Elisha rescues the situation. Some elements are worth singling out:

The assumption that the king of Syria is making an impossible demand in order to provoke a quarrel is perfectly consistent with the psychology of kings, both ancient and modern.

Naaman's anger at Elisha's simple response is also perfectly comprehensible. We expect the Word of God to come with external authenticating criteria. (It rarely does.) But only those who are willing to follow its simplest commands will experience its power to save.

The point of the whole is summed up in v. 15b: The God of Israel is the God of all the earth. Here we meet Jonah again. Not the God of Western culture or American glory or transnational power. But the God of all the earth. Elisha is a servant, and he is an Israelite. But God is more compassionate, more loving, more concerned for the suffering beyond Israel's borders than most Israelites would have expected.

So Elisha refuses the money (v. 16) because he understands the riches inherent in his vocation. Neither this nor Elisha's remarkably realistic compromise with absolute principle (in vv. 18f.) is included in the lectionary readings proper. But either could well be used as a sermon topic or an illustration on another occasion.

SECOND LESSON: 1 CORINTHIANS 9:24-27

At this point in the Corinthian letter Paul, who has made himself a slave in the service of others (9:19), shifts the metaphor to the world of athletics. He is still talking about his own ministry, which he sees as an example for all Christians (11:1).

While the references are general—athletic contests took place in many cities in Greece—the Corinthian games were watched with special interest throughout the Greek-speaking world, and Paul's metaphors are as familiar to his Corinthian readers as similar figures were to most residents of Los Angeles during the 1984 Olympics.

Greek athletic competition was arduous. Participants could not compete without stating under oath that they had trained for at least ten months; many trained for a lifetime. The physical development was outstanding, as is evident from the musculature in some Greek statues, which came from living models (well before the invention of Nautilus training). The athletic level, even when allowance is made for the difficulty of exact translation, was clearly very high. (For example, the long jump record—which involved carrying heavy stones that were flung backward at the moment of takeoff—was apparently something over fifty feet.) In most games, winners were given money. But in the isthmic games at Corinth (and in some others) the winner earned a wreath (cf. 1 Tim. 4:8; 1 Pet. 5:4)—and lifelong fame. Paul takes his metaphors from two of the best-known events: running and boxing.

V. 24, as often with Paul and even very good modern preachers, includes a sermon illustration gone awry. In races, only one contestant receives a prize; in the Christian life, all do. Yet the point is clear. Would the illustration be as effective if, like the Dodo in *Alice in Wonderland,* he had democratized the competitive metaphor and insisted that everybody has won, and *all* must have prizes? It does not bother Paul—or any sensible reader—that in athletics training precedes participation, while in the Christian life the two are simultaneous. But the price the athlete must pay for competence, v. 25 reminds us, is discipline, continence. (Sexual continence, vs. both ancient and modern prejudice, seems to be unrelated to athletic performance. But discipline with regard to, say, food and drink is necessary.)

The contrast between the perishable wreath and the imperishable one is clear and striking. When all has been said that needs saying about a theology of the cross (as against a theology of glory), most Christians, especially those for whom life is hard, need the promise that suffering is not the last word. God does not promise only a crown; but a crown is included in the promise.

In v. 26 Paul shifts the emphasis. The picture now is of an aimless runner, one with no goal, or a shadowboxer, one who always wins because he has no real opposition. (Incidentally, the Greeks, who had a word for everything, also had a word for shadowboxing: *skiamachia.*) What would one make of a runner who, midway in a race, decided to run across the fields instead of down the track, say, on the theory that it might prove to be more interesting? No time is allowed for "finding oneself" in the race of life as Paul understands it; one finds oneself in the course of doing.

For finally, Paul insists (v. 27), it is possible to fail in the course one has taken. A hard body is needed for really strenuous effort. And Paul himself, whose goal is to preach to others (now the metaphor disappears) might, if insufficiently disciplined, turn out to be *adokimos*, unacceptable, tested but not approved, disqualified—in Olympic metaphor, eliminated in a trial heat.

Clearly the notion of the strenuousness of the Christian life can be, and has been, overdrawn. In this picture there is no room for laughter, for relaxation, for study and thought, for listening, for self-forgetful service.

But are these not adequately provided for in most of our churches? Might we not be so busily engaged in these more comfortable aspects of the Chrsitian life that we forget that the Adversary is still at work, seeking someone to devour (1 Pet. 5:8)? The warning of v. 27 might well apply to us if we refuse to offer, especially to the young, any challenge sufficiently serious to warrant a significant response.

GOSPEL: MARK 1:40–45

This reading returns to the theme of leprosy. If we look for connections with the other readings, we might ask what the three principals are required to do. Naaman is given a very pedestrian task. Paul is assigned the heroic self-discipline of a well-trained athlete. And the leper of our story is hardly required to do anything at all. Clearly God's power is more central than human response.

Our pericope is the third specific healing in Mark 1. Here no description of the illness beyond the somewhat vague term "leper/leprosy" is given. Otherwise, the details fit the standard healing pattern noted by form criticism: (1) the meeting of the sick person and the healer, (2) the request for healing, (3) the healing itself, here accompanied by both an action ("stretched out . . . and touched") and a word, (4) the proof of the healing, and (5) the response of the crowd. Some Markan touches are also included.

Basic to the understanding of this event in ancient terms is the

terror with which leprosy itself was viewed, epitomized in the slogan,
"Leprosy is a living death." (Cf. Job 18:13: leprosy is the "firstborn
of death.") The right exercised in 2:5 ("My son, your sins are for-
given") is already anticipated in the healing; whoever is capable of the
one is worthy of the other. (Note the king's question in 2 Kings 5:7:
"Am I God, to kill and to make alive?")

In v. 40 the leper comes to Jesus. Forbidden entry to Jerusalem by
rabbinic regulations and subject to a variety of biblical laws (Lev.
13—14), lepers were still to be found in many towns and villages. This
individual knows enough of Jesus' reputation to seek him out, con-
vinced that Jesus is able to help if he is willing. Note that in this verse
the famous problem of pain is already posed: God (here: Jesus) is able
to deal with suffering, but is he willing? No satisfactory abstract
answer to this question has ever been given. And, concretely, the
person who finds no help is left with the problem still unresolved. In
our text, however, a Christian way of seeing the question is illustrated:
every instance which shows God to be both willing and able to help is
a promise that all other instances, too, are ultimately remediable. The
problem exists only because our experience of God's goodness leads
us to expect what we do not always see. If the universe were meaning-
less, neither joy nor pain would be problematic.

In v. 41, some texts say that Jesus was moved to anger rather than
pity. Though the reading is poorly attested, it has some claim to
authenticity. If it is correct, it reflects anger at the disease and all it
represents, not at the leper's request. The emotional involvement of
the healer with the one to be healed is everywhere presumed in the
first century. (Cf. John 11:33, 35). The God of Scripture is no cool
Aristotelian Prime Mover. Perhaps that is one reason early Christians
(and Jews) found the indifferent (untroubled) gods of the Epicureans
incomprehensible; in the Talmud an *Epikoros* is, for all practical
purposes, simply an atheist.

That Jesus wills to save is indicated by his gestures as well as his
words: he stretches out his hand (cf. Exod. 7:5; 14:16, 21; 15:12) and
touches (cf. 2 Kings 5:11) the leper. The healing (v. 42) is, as commonly in miracles, immediate.

What follows, read simply as narrative, is peculiar. Solemnly
charged to say nothing (v. 44), the healed man immediately disobeys
the command. Clearly, a theological reading of the text is demanded,

since Mark cannot have intended to stress the man's disobedience. The various motifs are apparent: (1) the command to silence, as often in Mark, shows that Jesus, though filled with divine power, is one who wishes to be known not by power but by suffering (8:30–33; 10:43–45); (2) Jesus' power, however, cannot be contained; (3) though Jesus wills no conflict with the priests (v. 44), his enemies are already forming against him (2:1—3:6).

What kind of "testimony" (v. 44, RSV: "proof") is this? One translation is negative: "as a witness against them" (either: the priests or the people). Another is more positive: "a demonstration for them." A decision between the two is hardly possible. In any case, it is important to remember that "all miracles are ambiguous." That God could cure an incurable disease like leprosy is, taken alone, very hard to believe. But for the God who can save even preachers, to do so is a mere trifle.

The Seventh Sunday After the Epiphany

Lutheran	Roman Catholic	Episcopal	Pres/UCC/Chr	Meth/COCU
Isa. 43:18–25	Isa. 43:18–19, 21–22, 24b–25	Isa. 43:18–25	Isa. 43:18–25	Isa. 43:15–25
2 Cor. 1:18–22	2 Cor. 1:18–22	2 Cor. 1:18–22	2 Cor. 1:18–22	2 Cor. 1:18–22
Mark 2:1–12	Mark 2:1–12	Mark 2:1–12	Mark 2:1–12	Mark 2:1–12

FIRST LESSON: ISAIAH 43:18–25

In this chapter we find one of the most striking metaphors anywhere in the poetry of the OT: a new —almost an inverse—Exodus.

The first Exodus is noted in the great words in 43:1: "Fear not, for I have redeemed you. I have called you by name, you are mine." God has "created" Jacob, "formed" Israel, and been with them in trials by both water and fire (43:2). "I, I alone am the Lord, and besides me there is no Savior" (43:11). This great God, like a mighty warrior, has made a path in the sea in which chariots and horses and the whole massed Egyptian army are lost, "quenched like a wick" (v. 17). Now in v. 18 God tells them to forget all of this. For he will do a new thing, making, not dry land in the midst of water, but waters in the midst of dry land. Why? Not because they deserve it, but because he is that kind of God (vv. 22–25).

Isaiah has earlier promised that God will bring the people home through a wilderness transformed by plentiful water (41:17–20); now the promise is graphically described in terms of a counter-Exodus. Nowhere perhaps is more clearly stated the OT view that nature is completely subject to the will of God, a conception that survives today largely in the pitiful harshness of those who view natural calamities as acts of divine vengeance. For Isaiah, God acts for the redemption of the people.

"Do not remember" (v. 18) implies "Do not allow your memories of what has been to obscure what I am about to do." The Exodus, like every great experience of God, can—perversely—become an obstacle to trusting in God for present or future help. In the youth musical *Tell It Like It Is*, the young singers admit that the past is interesting and probably important, but "please stop talkin' 'bout the good ol' days," they sing, "'cause they'll never be back again." Each new generation needs hope of its own. Has the church forgotten how to teach people, especially young people, to hope?

In v. 19 the question "Do you not perceive it?" is rhetorical: "Surely you can see it!" The "path in the waters" of v. 16 is now countered with a "path in the wilderness," the "way in the sea" with "rivers in the desert" (v. 18). The animals (possibly wolves and owls) in v. 20 honor God, not for improving their lot, but for caring for the people. They join in singing "Hallelujah" with the chosen people (v. 21). Faithfulness in redemption is faithfulness in creation as well, so the creation honors the Redeemer.

But the people of God exhibit no corresponding faithfulness. On the contrary, they substitute religion for God. The text probably does not charge that they have ignored sacrifice, which would be unlike a prophet. More probably it suggests that the people have been zealous, even over-zealous, in offering sacrifices, but they have been unconcerned for God (v. 22) or godly living (v. 24), performing religious acts for someone or something other than God.

This theme can easily become cheap. It is not true that our churches are filled with hypocritical religionists, that our young people have no sense of the love of God, that all true piety is to be found outside the church (and in the hearts of a tiny minority of clergy!). And yet, religious activity is no guarantor of faith. We all, perhaps especially the clergy, need to be reminded of that.

For, in the wonderful counterpart to the confession of v. 11, the concluding verse of our lesson reads, "I, I am He who blots out your transgression for my own sake." The world needs our work and witness and shames us for failing to provide it. But our sin and folly do not change the Creator/Redeemer's faithfulness.

SECOND LESSON: 2 CORINTHIANS 1:18–22

If somehow I were given an opportunity of worshiping with several early Christian churches, the list to be drawn up at my own pleasure, the church at Corinth would almost certainly be dead last. There is something almost eerie about this congregation and what they are willing to say about Paul, through whose preaching they themselves became Christians. (So much for their "wisdom.")

In our text the accusation is apparently fickleness. While the details are obscure and differently interpreted, 1:16 most naturally implies that Paul intended to visit Corinth twice, once on the way to Macedonia and again on the return trip from Macedonia to Judea. For some reason he changed his plans. And like pouting children (or parents) the Corinthians seem to have wailed, "but you *promised!*" They then accuse Paul of unreliability.

So Paul argues (1:12, 17) that he makes plans, not on the basis of his own vacillating spirit, but on the basis of God's grace. The charge that he is undependable, saying both yes and no at the same time, is met by one of the most fascinating digressions anywhere in Scripture. God, he insists (v. 18), will bear witness that Paul does not say whatever will be to his advantage. This in turn leads him to a discussion, not of his life (which determined opponents could always find a way of misunderstanding), but of the heart of his message: God's faithfulness in Jesus Christ.

It might be well to stop here to reflect on this defense. Paul must have been as sensitive to slander as any of the rest of us. But for the sake of the truth of the gospel he shifts the argument to the heart of the

matter: has he preached an ambiguous gospel? His personal reputation is not very important. For Jesus Christ, Paul says, is God's yes to
us. Everything else is ambiguous: life itself, our motives, the interpretation of Scripture, language about God, the results of particular
programs in church or society, personal relationships, the impact of
historical movements (missionary, revolutionary, technological)—
the list is endless, and no imaginative preacher will have to look far for
examples which any specific congregation will acknowledge as their
own dilemmas. But at one point, Jesus Christ himself, God, speaks a
clear yes. Not yes and no, but yes. All the promises of God are
fulfilled. Adam, Noah, Abraham, Moses, David, the prophets—
whatever was promised to and in them finds its fulfillment in Jesus
Christ.

Thus the "Amen" (may it be so) is pronounced to the glory of God
through Jesus Christ (v. 20). Christians are thus confirmed (the root of
Amen seems to imply solidity, firmness, reliability) by God: established in Christ, they are commissioned (literally, made to share
Christ's anointing), sealed (a reference to baptism is possible but not
very likely), and given a guarantee in the Spirit. The verb Paul uses for
establish (bebaioō) in v. 21 is a commercial term for confirmation. The
noun translated "guarantee" *(arrabōn)* in v. 22 means "first install-
ment," not partial payment (the Spirit is given in fullness), but promise. (In modern Greek it is the word for *engagement ring.*)

Three motifs from this reading might be emphasized for sermonic
purposes. The first is the way Paul answers attacks on his person by
setting forth the theological basis of his life. Like Paul, the church can
be attacked on many grounds. But since we preach, not ourselves, but
Jesus Christ as Lord (2 Cor. 4:5), the criticism is ultimately irrelevant
(however it may shame us); the truth of the message is avoided, not
evaluated, by such charges.

The second motif for preaching is, obviously, the promise of God.
In our text, 1:20, "promises" is plural. In Acts 2:39; 13:32; 26:6; and
occasionally in Paul's letters (Rom. 4:13, 14, 16; 9:8; Gal. 3:17, 22)
promise is singular, almost a technical term. The OT, then, is not so
much a series of individual promises as promise itself, a promise
fulfilled in Christ.

The third preaching theme might be broadly Trinitarian. God,
Christ, and the Spirit are all related to the fulfillment of God's promise
through Christ, sealed by the Spirit. Just as we need a full canon of

Scripture, not a single book (or author), so we need Father, Son, and Spirit lest an overemphasis on any one of the three persons skew our understanding of the God who promises.

GOSPEL: MARK 2:1–12

This reading begins the next section of Mark (2:1—3:6), the theme of which is the authority of Jesus, set forth primarily in a series of conflicts with opponents, possibly in terms of ever increasing hostility (2:6, 16, 18, 24; 3:2, 6). Our section (2:1–12) is a combination of a miracle story (2:1–5, 11–12) and a controversy-discourse (2:6–10), which suggests that behind our narrative are two originally independent stories. The double "he said to the paralytic" (vv. 5, 10) and the awkwardness of the insertion in v. 10 show that the narrative has undergone some expansion.

The usual miracle form is reflected, with some traits appropriate to this special context. Thus the seriousness of the illness (cf. 5:3–5) or the difficulty of the healing (cf. 9:23–24) gives way to the difficulty of bringing Jesus and the paralytic together; hence the dramatic detail about the roof. (Roofs, a combination of poles, reeds, branches, and mud, were often left partially unfinished during the dry season so that grain and other materials could be brought in. Irreparable damage to the roof is not implied.) The word of healing (v. 11) is preceded by the word of forgiveness (v. 5), not because illness is caused by sin (the NT does not encourage this view, common in the ancient world; see John 5:14; 9:2–3), but for the purposes of the narrative, in which forgiveness is the archetypal miracle; see also Ps. 103:3. (Most people probably agree with Heinrich Heine: "God will forgive me—that's His job!") The proof of the miracle is given in his walking out with the pallet, the crowd's amazement in the concluding quotation.

That Jesus was preaching (the word) is part of the Markan portrait (1:2, 14, 21). Whatever variations in terminology occur in these passages, it is important to note that early Christianity thought of both Jesus' ministry and their own mission in terms of a word to be proclaimed. No facile comments on the demise of neo-orthodoxy can obscure the fact that at this point the theology dominant in the fifties had seized upon a profoundly biblical note which we ignore at our peril.

Yet since the fifties we have also learned how "believing" the word is inevitably a compound of faith and action. Here, too, our text may have gone before us. The four determined friends, thwarted by the crowd at the door, climb the outside stairway and remove part of the roof to let the man down. Jesus, *seeing their faith,* then sets the healing into motion. (The parallels in 2:8 and 14:4, 6 may suggest, however, that insight, not action, is the point here.) Narrative permits the preacher to include the various participants in the sermon, so this point may properly be stressed. If the text is used as a model of evangelism, it might be noted that the four friends disappear once this act of faith has been performed; of the "subjective benefits" of their actions we know nothing. Faith is present, though it is not, as in many miracle stories, central.

What is central in the story in its present form is the controversy set off by v. 5b. Technically, the scribes are right; God alone can forgive sins. Jesus is also right; neither the forgiveness of sins nor the healing of the lame is possible (vv. 9–10). What is true and important is not limited to what is possible. That is the whole point of miracles.

Some sermonic attention might be given to the forgiveness of sins: why a paralytic would need it, why we don't believe we need it but believe that those who do need it don't deserve it, what it might mean at any level higher than the individual, what it implies for parents, executives, political leaders, or preachers, and above all what it means that the forgiveness of sins is the prerogative of God alone.

That the man is described as paralyzed, not lame (cf. Isa. 35:6), and that the cry in v. 12 is not specifically christological shows that our text is still comparatively undeveloped. The modern preacher, of course, may develop it, since reflection on the text is part of the preacher's calling. V. 12 already points in this direction; the individual miracle, by its transcendent power, hints at the power of the one who does all that follows in the gospel.

That early Christian controversy lies behind our text is clear. The disciples were no more given answers to all their theological questions in the original encounter with Jesus than we are. Hence the question of whether and how he forgives our sins and heals our diseases must be decided as we continually encounter Jesus as risen Lord.

The Eighth Sunday After the Epiphany

Lutheran	Roman Catholic	Episcopal	Pres/UCC/Chr	Meth/COCU
Hos. 2:14–16, (17–18) 19–20	Hos. 2:14b, 15b, 19–20	Hos. 2:14–23	Hos. 2:14–20	Hos. 2:14–23
2 Cor. 3:1b–6	2 Cor. 3:1–6	2 Cor. 3:(4–11) 17—4:2	2 Cor. 3:17—4:2	2 Cor. 3:1b–6
Mark 2:18–22	Mark 2:18–22	Mark 2:18–22	Mark 2:18–22	Mark 2:18–22

FIRST LESSON: HOSEA 2:14–23

The three readings for this Sunday are all in some way polemic. In the Hosea passage, as throughout the book, the argument is carried out in an elaborate series of occasionally obscure but often striking metaphors.

Oddly enough, in the midst of a theological tradition adamantly opposed to any connection between sexual imagery and God, this early prophet takes over several sexual images from Baal worship to denounce the "harlotry" of Israel. The reason is evident. If one would speak of peace and justice and hope and wisdom, images lie ready to hand from a dozen facets of human experience. But if one's theme is a passionate concern for a loving and faithful Creator, many images are simply much too pale and ineffectual.

Israel's harlotry in following Baal—whose worship concentrated on fertility themes—provides the immediate focus of our section. Israel has burned incense to Baal in thanksgiving for the "vines and fig trees" which Baal worship seems to have produced. ("Hire" in 2:12 and 9:1 is the prostitute's *fee*.) For thus "forgetting" Yahweh (v. 13), she will be punished as the fields once more are abandoned to wild animals (v. 12). But in our section the emphasis is on the Lord's plan to win back the wife whose love he has lost. If disaster will lead her to forsake her other loves (vv. 6–13), God will also set about to "allure" (the equivalent of "seduce," as in Exod. 22:16) Israel (v. 14a), to bring her again into the wilderness where, as a young bride, she had earlier followed God (v. 14b; cf. Jer. 2:2). He will "speak to her heart" (v. 14c), that is, woo her tenderly, like a young lover. The first fine careless rapture of the early days in salvation-history, the Exodus, will be restored (v. 15).

Vv. 16–23 are a rapid-fire succession of images, with several changes of pronoun (she/her, you, them). "In that day" (vv. 16, 18, 21) suggests the day of God's decisive action, when idolatry will be forgotten and the false Baals no longer worshiped (vv. 16, 17), when a covenant of peace will be established, encompassing both animals (cf. 4:3) and all those who would make war (v. 18).

In vv. 19f. the betrothal imagery recurs. As bride-price, God will promise and provide five things: righteousness, justice, steadfast love, mercy, and faithfulness—all "forever." (Cf. our "as long as you both shall live.") These are a complete restoration of that covenant which Israel's faithlessness had shattered.

In the final verses (vv. 21–23) God returns to the Baal metaphor, promising again all those things the fertility cult of Baal had seemed to ensure. The symbolic names of Hosea's children (1:4, 6, 9) are now reversed, and each becomes a part of the promise; God again affirms Israel as "my people," and Israel acknowledges the Lord as "my God."

Many studies of Hosea have concentrated on the extraordinary relationships between Hosea and his wife, on the metaphor of the adulterous spouse rather than on its referent. But what if the love of God really is as Hosea portrays it? What if our faithlessness does not negate God's faithfulness? This is Hosea's question to us.

It is easy, of course, for the preacher to turn even such questions into clichés, to encourage a mentality in which our assurance of God's intention to save becomes irredeemably smug. Furthermore, direct homiletic application of such a theme is not easy.

But then neither is preaching. And without helping to develop in the congregation over years of worship and service an awareness of the white-hot faithfulness of God, no preacher can hope to be genuinely heard. People who agree on particular issues may follow our lead in individual instances. But they will not have heard the word of God. And they will feel free to dissent not only when we are wrong but also whenever it is more comfortable to do so. Without God, religion is just not worth getting excited about.

SECOND LESSON: 2 CORINTHIANS 3:1–6

This section of 2 Corinthians is, like so much of the letter, taken up with a defense of Paul's ministry and apostleship. But just what Paul's opponents said about him is not clear. Apparently the leaders Paul attacked were in some way related to Judaism, Gnosticism, and the Hellenistic conception of *theioi andres,* divine men filled with the power of the Spirit. (The three are by no means mutually exclusive.) They may have claimed to be "sufficient," possibly using concepts or terminology related to the Septuagint's (mis)translation of El Shaddai as *ho hikanos,* [the Sufficient One]. In 2:17 Paul suggests that they are not sincere, that they "peddle" God's word. (The term implies both *adulteration* and *for profit,* as for example, in adding water to wine. A similar practice in nineteenth-century America led to Oliver Wendell Holmes's whimsical legal comment, "Sometimes circumstantial evidence is very strong—as when you find a trout in the milk!") Paul and his co-workers, on the other hand, know that that word comes from God.

Paul's opponents, to be sure, have put him in a dilemma. If he does not respond to their slanders, he might be thought guilty. If he does, he will certainly be considered smug and self-righteous. (Hence the rhetorical question in v. 3a.) In answering, Paul neatly turns the tables on those who belittle him.

Letters of recommendation were common among both Jews and Gentiles in the ancient world. Paul himself recognizes such letters (1 Cor. 16:3) and commends friends to other churches (Rom. 16:1; 1 Cor. 16:10, 15f.; 2 Cor. 8:22–24; Phil. 2:25–30; Philem. 10). So, he says his opponents bring letters of recommendation to Corinth and take them along when they leave for new fields (v. 1). But Paul has no need of such letters in Corinth, whose members became Christians through his ministry. (Note the language of v. 3: the letter is *from* Christ, written *with* the Spirit of the living God. Paul is merely the "supplier.") These living letters are not private but open to public scrutiny.

Because Paul is a theologian-preacher, however, he cannot remain content with this *ad hominem* argument. His language contrasts tablets of stone (Exod. 24:12; 31:18; 32:15–16) with "tablets" of human hearts. (Cf. the new covenant of Jer. 31:31–33, a thought that he will develop in vv. 4–18.)

In v. 4 Paul deals with the first of the two issues entangled throughout our section: the validity of his own apostolic mission. (The second, the relationship between the old and new covenants, occupies the rest of the chapter.) Paul makes a very bold claim: the *exercising* of apostolic gifts shows the *presence* of such gifts. (In our day, this is the conclusive argument for the ordination of women.) In a peculiar way Paul can thus assert his "confidence"—but not in himself so much as through Christ before God. In essence, Paul responds to his opponents' claim to sufficiency: Sufficiency, yes; self-sufficiency, no.

Both sides of this claim are important. On the one hand, no Christian is sufficient for the task assigned. On the other, God is. A mildly cynical Canadian friend once gave me his explanation of the fact that in his country church attendance is so much higher on Christmas and Easter than on any other Sundays: "Of course—those are the Sundays when you can go to church and be pretty sure of hearing something about God!"

Finally it is God alone who is sufficient. This thought now leads Paul to a discussion of the letter and the Spirit. This contrast can hardly be intended—though it is often so interpreted—to distinguish biblical literalism from a "higher" form of religion. For Paul the Law is good, the Bible (as for all pious Jews in the first century) an expression of the will of God. But any good thing can, divorced from the Spirit of the God who gave it, become an instrument of the purely human and thus a "dispensation of death." Anyone, by denying the Lord who is the Spirit, can make the new covenant a mere variation on the old. Finally, *homo religiosus* is a threat to faith. This is the real difference between Paul and his opponents.

The problem is by no means an antiquarian one. In every age ways of substituting piety or the Bible or the Church (or aversion to piety, antifundamentalism, and hostility to the Church) for the life giving Spirit can be found.

GOSPEL: MARK 2:18–22

This reading includes three metaphors: the bridegroom, the patched garment, and the wine and wineskins. In the Markan context, all three address the issues raised by the question of fasting.

The scene as Mark sets it is somewhat artificial. Some kind of fast is being observed by John's disciples and by (the disciples of) the Pharisees that Jesus' disciples apparently do not observe. Since Jesus and the disciples, as pious Jews, surely did keep "the fast" required on the Day of Atonement (Acts 27:9; cf. Lev. 16:29; Num. 29:7), the reference is probably to some special practice observed by some Jews but not others. Jesus explains their conduct by asking, "Can the wedding guests fast while the bridegroom is with them?"

In this form the question points to a key aspect of Jesus' teaching: the presence of the kingdom in his own ministry. Fasting—a symbol of mourning—is incompatible with the joy the kingdom brings. At least one scholar has consequently posited an original shorter form of Jesus' response: Can wedding guests fast?

Problems become evident, however, when one continues with the form we now have. "While the bridegroom is with them" not only includes an early Christian symbol which Jesus did not use for himself; it also indicates a temporary situation, one which is focused, not on the joy of the kingdom, but on the presence of Jesus. It implies what vv. 19b–20 spell out in detail: Jesus will die, and after his death the custom of fasting will be reintroduced. The passage has now become an explanation of the temporary abandonment of fasting and a justification of its reintroduction into the life of the early church. The original dispute has gotten swallowed up by a prophecy of Jesus' coming death. (See also 3:6.)

Some scholars therefore posit a pre-Markan text in which vv. 21ff. were attached directly to v. 19a. Then the question of Jesus' conduct is answered by three metaphors about "incompatible" things, of which fasting and the joy of the wedding form the first.

The second pair of incompatible things is the unshrunk cloth and the old garment. Since shrinkage of up to ten percent was not uncommon, any but the loosest of clothing would become unwearable unless material for patching had been washed several times before being sown onto a tear or a hole. And new wine, if put into skins which had already been stretched by previous use, would ferment and burst the old skins.

But what do the metaphors mean? One interpretation contrasts Jesus and his message as the "new" thing and Jewish tradition as the "old" thing. In its most extreme form, it would be saying that no Jewish practice ought to be included in "pure" Christianity—a Gnostic teaching perfectly reflected in the nonsensical form of the metaphor in the Gospel of Thomas (Saying 47): "No one sews an *old* patch on a *new* garment, because a rip will result." Here a statement objectively false—a rip will not result—has been created by mangling a metaphor in order to separate Christianity from its Jewish roots; its secondary nature is as obvious as its perverse theology.

A better interpretation, therefore, is not to allegorize the cloth and the wine but to ask what the incompatibility of "old" and "new" might intend. In its original form, the metaphor must have urged conduct consonant with the new thing—the kingdom of God—ushered in by Jesus' ministry. Inevitably, as time went on, this insight became elaborated to contrast Judaism and Christianity, to the depreciation and disadvantage of the former.

For contemporary preaching it is surely better to put the argument once more within the framework of the temptations faced by the people of God. Some of these temptations, to be sure, involve a contrast between "traditionalism" and "creativity," between old familiar habits and the new Christian life style. As the Lukan parallel (Luke 5:39) reminds us, however, the new can be *worse* than the old as well as *better*. Carlyle's scornful political summary—"Whigs stumbling blindly forward, Tories holding blindly back"—reminds us that no ideological preference for either the good old days or some imagined glorious future can possibly substitute for wisdom and integrity in doing the will of God in every new day.

The Transfiguration of Our Lord
The Last Sunday After the Epiphany

Lutheran	Roman Catholic	Episcopal	Pres/UCC/Chr	Meth/COCU
2 Kings 2:1–12a	Dan. 7:9–10, 13–14	1 Kings 19:9–18	Dan. 7:13–14	2 Kings 2:1–12a
2 Cor. 3:12—4:2	2 Pet. 1:16–19	2 Pet. 1:16–19 (20–21)	Rev. 1:4–8	2 Cor. 3:12—4:2
Mark 9:2–9	Mark 9:2–10	Mark 9:2–9	John 18:33–37	Mark 9:5–9

FIRST LESSON: 2 KINGS 2:1–12a

It is a sign of the times that more people in the average congregation will be familiar with the movie *Chariots of Fire* than with our present lesson, which provided the metaphor. Elijah, the great prophet whose running battle with King Ahab forms the major theme in the latter part of 1 Kings, is about to depart; his place will be taken by Elisha, under whom Elijah's goals (the end of Omri's dynasty and of his alliances with Phoenician states) are finally reached. The chariots of fire present when he is taken up by the whirlwind are understood by the writers of 2 Kings as representing the power Elijah exercised— equivalent to a whole cavalry of Israel's troops (cf. 2 Kings 13:14).

The section begins (2:1) with an indication that the time for Elijah's departure has come. His work as the successor of Moses, preserving the integrity of the people against foreign gods and influence, is done. So he and Elisha, his successor-to-be, leave Gilgal for Bethal (v. 2), Jericho (v. 4), and the region of the Jordan (v. 6). The extended narrative makes it clear that God—not merely Elijah—intends Elisha as Elijah's true successor. The Moses motif is especially clear in the parting of the waters (vv. 8, 14), in which first Elijah then Elisha show themselves to be in the succession of the great lawgiver, the preserver of the purity of the true people of God.

The whirlwind (vv. 1, 11) is a common phenomenon in the Near East and suggests both power and the Spirit (*ruah*) of God. (Trivia buffs will note that Elijah was not taken up by a fiery chariot; he was taken up by the whirlwind, accompanied by horsemen and chariots, vv. 11–12).

Three times (vv. 2, 4, 6) Elijah asks Elisha to leave him; twice (vv. 3, 5) the sons of the prophets hint that it might be well for him to go somewhere else. With a solemn oath (vv. 2, 4, 6) Elisha refuses, presumably passing the test the Lord had set for him through the other prophets.

It might be well to stop at this point and note how much more complicated it is to be a prophet than some contemporary rhetoric suggests. The guilds of prophets, to whom the kings looked for advice about the will of God (1 Kings 22:6), were often wrong. The lone prophets usually proclaimed disaster and were usually right. But they did so with the assurance, not that they were better informed, but simply that God had spoken to them. Any sensible prophet today favors alliances, reconciliation, peace making, just as the house of Omri did. Elijah, on the other hand (and Elisha after him), was concerned only that foreign influences, especially foreign religious influences, be removed root and branch from Israel. So sensible a prophetic notion as a verifiable nuclear freeze, for example, was beyond their ken not simply technologically but theologically. The general principle of the Deuteronomic view of history—that God rewards good and punishes evil—is unusually ambiguous today, and the prophetic aspect of the preacher's calling must live precisely with that ambiguity.

So Elijah shows that he is a man of God and a successor of Moses by parting the waters (v. 8). Elisha, who would be in the same line, asks Elijah for a double portion of his prophetic spirit, which of course is not Elijah's to grant. But what he cannot do, God can. So Elisha is confirmed in his vocation by God; first he sees Elijah as he is taken up (v. 12) and then he repeats the Mosaic miracle with the use of Elijah's mantle (vv. 13, 14). And he too is likened to the chariots of Israel and its horseman (2 Kings 13:14).

Sermons from this lesson might emphasize the unshakable confidence in the will of God against all earthly power (as in the movie, when a Scottish missionary-to-be chooses the will of God over the wishes of his prince and future king). In connection with the next two readings the question naturally arises, Where is the Mosaic tradition to be found?

SECOND LESSON: 2 CORINTHIANS 3:12—4:2

Even the most casual reader can see that this passage is essentially a sermon on the shining of Moses' face in Exod. 34:29–35. *Splendor* (glory, *doxa*) is used thirteen times between 3:7 and 4:6 (in 3:7, 8, 9, 10, 11, 18; 4:4, 6).

The "hope" of v. 12 rests on the splendor of the new covenant and produces great boldness, which Paul contrasts with Moses, who, he says, veiled his face in order that the people might not see the fading glory (or: the fading *of* the glory) on his face. The contrast with the openness of Paul's ministry is clear.

The next verses elaborate the notion of the veil. Note that Paul here, as always, speaks highly of the Law. Yet the Law fails because the veil that Moses interposed between the divine splendor and the people's vision is now interposed between the reading of the old covenant and the hearts of the hearers. In Christ, and only in Christ (vv. 14, 16), the veil is removed. Since the reading of Scripture was an important part of every synagogue service, the condemnation here is not so much of individual Jews as of Judaism itself; only the lifting of the veil through Christ makes possible a true understanding of the Scripture. He and he alone is the hermeneutical center for Paul, whatever exegetical methods he may use on particular texts.

V. 16, which is nearly impossibly to translate, is a reinterpretation of Exod. 34:34; it seems to mean that whenever anyone *converts*, God removes the veil. And, as always in Paul, this allowing oneself to be acted upon by the Spirit is understood as freedom (v. 17; cf. Rom. 8:2, 21; 1 Cor. 9:1, 19; Gal. 2:4; 4:31; 5:1, 13).

That Paul twice (vv. 17, 18) identifies "the Lord" and "the Spirit" need not detain us. An explicit Trinitarian theology is not to be expected as early as Paul, yet it is equally clear from passages like Rom. 8:9–11 and 2 Cor. 13:14 that Paul was no Binitarian. He thinks here in functional terms, the contrast of 3:6 (between the letter and the Spirit) in his mind. It is Christ, whose glory we all behold, who transfers us from the dispensation of death to the dispensation of life.

In v. 18 "reflecting" rather than "beholding" is a possible translation of the rare Greek verb, but the word seems to stress what Christians see, not what we are. This seeing results in a real transformation (v. 18). The Orthodox concept of *theiosis*, according to which believers are eventually divinized, reflects a Greek indifference to the infinite distance between the divine and the human; it must be admitted, however, that this verse already points in a similar direction. We see, though in a mirror; we are transformed, though never to the infinite stage of glory in which God dwells.

Those who think of Paul as a crabbed misanthrope might do well to ponder the depth of religious feeling in these verses. Oral Roberts tells of the time when, as a young man, he came across his father reading the Bible, with tears streaming down his cheeks. "Dad," he asked, "why are you crying?" "Oral," his father replied, "some day you'll know." Paul knew.

In 4:1–12 Paul turns from Moses' ministry to his own. The polemic opposition to his detractors comes once more to the fore as he insists that he has been called by the mercy of God, that he does not neglect his duty (RSV: lose heart), and that (unlike those whose shameful practices adulterate the gospel) he speaks the truth openly to all. His commendation, as in 3:2f., is to be found in the response of the Corinthian believers to his preaching of the word of God (4:2).

Most of us are quite uncomfortable with the notion that some do not believe the gospel because God has somehow blinded their hearts. But the alternative—if the question *must* be asked—is often unconsciously to judge the non-Christian neighbor as less intelligent or less morally sensitive than those of us who believe the gospel. In this light, perhaps allowing the "mystery of unbelief" to remain a mystery is not a bad idea.

If one wishes to preach on Christ as the fulfiller of the Mosaic tradition, as in all three of this Sunday's lessons, one should be very careful to be positive (Moses is our spiritual ancestor), not negative (Moses represents modern Judaism). The removing of the veil of unbelief, Paul reminds us, is an act not of our wit or virtue but of God's mercy.

GOSPEL: MARK 9:2–10

Our verses are the climax of the central section of Mark: Peter's confession (8:27–30), followed by the first passion-prediction (8:31), Peter's rebuke of Jesus (8:32), the rebuke of Peter by Jesus (8:33), a brief comment on the nature of discipleship (8:34–38), an eschatological prediction (9:1), and the Transfiguration (9:2–8), concluding in the command to silence (9:9–10). The key question is, Who is Jesus?

The best explanation of the "after six days" of v. 2 is that it is an eschatological symbol: "Rest on the seventh day is a sign of the resurrection in the age to come" (Apoc. Mos. 43:1; see also Exod. 24:16f.). The "high mountain," as often in the Scripture, is the place of revelation. (Cf. Exod. 19:3; 1 Kings 19:8; Gen. 22:2, 14.) Revelation, not the sharing of opinions, produces the truth about Jesus' nature.

The theme of glory is typically apocalyptic, characteristic of the heavenly realm in which Jesus' true nature shines forth. The themes of Dan. 12:3 and Exod. 34:29–35 are developed. Similar symbolism can be found in the resurrection accounts (Mark 16:5) and elsewhere (Rev. 3:4; 7:9, 13–14; 19:14; 20:11); the heavenly realm is already pointed to in the phrase "no fuller *on earth*. . . ." Yet this glimpse of Jesus' heavenly nature lies between 8:31 and 9:12, in which his suffering is stressed.

No clear Jewish tradition exists that both Elijah and Moses will return at the end of time, though this may be hinted at in Rev. 11:6. But both dwell in heaven and so are fit companions for the transfigured Jesus. Peter's suggestion in v. 5 is doubly foolish: Elijah and Moses are not part of the earthly realm, and Jesus cannot be held in this eschatological situation. The order—Jesus, Moses, Elijah—is probably, for Mark, an order of value.

In v. 6 Peter's confusion does no more than create nonsense; in 14:40 it will lead to Jesus' betrayal. In this instance Peter, like the women at the tomb (16:8), at least has the excuse that his bewilderment is produced by an epiphany, a direct manifestation of God. The overshadowing cloud (v. 7) also has antecedents in the Moses narrative (Exod. 24:15–18; 40:34–35).

Here, as in 1:11, Jesus is identified as God's "beloved Son." This phrase, like the command to "hear (= listen to and obey) him," alludes to Isa. 42:1; Ps. 2:7; Gen. 22:2, 12, 16; Deut. 18:15, all of which are understood to mean that Jesus alone is the saving, eschatological figure.

Continuity with the OT is an important NT theme. But it must never be understood as if Jesus were simply the culminating manifestation of God. The line has ended. As God's final word, he has no successors—only witnesses.

"Suddenly" the disciples are alone (v. 8), and they need instruction about the meaning of what they have witnessed; they are commanded to maintain their silence. If the command were intended only to point out that the divine is ineffable, the time-limitation ("until the Son of man should have risen from the dead") in v. 9 would be unnecessary. Nor does Elijah (vv. 11–13) simply point to a mystery. John the Baptist, as Elijah, has come, borne witness to Jesus—and been put to death. So the disciples may speak of the glory of the heavenly world, of Jesus' resurrected nature, at the appropriate time, namely, after the resurrection. Mark's point is not that the resurrection is peripheral, but that it cannot be dissociated from suffering and death—either Jesus' or ours.

Hence the discussion in v. 10 is not about the resurrection as such. As the context shows, the disciples are to witness to John, the suffering Elijah, not the exalted Elijah and Moses whom they have seen with Jesus. So, after the resurrection (16:8), the proclaimed word may include the Transfiguration, but only in the light of what it foreshadows: the resurrected life of the crucified one.

Sermonic themes almost leap from the page in these verses: glory, Moses and Elijah, Jesus' true nature, the ineffable world awaiting the disciples. In the context of Mark as a whole, however, these great themes are only one side of the coin. The other is service, suffering, crucifixion, and death. "No Cross, No Crown," "The Way of the

Cross Leads Home," "He became obedient unto death"—books, hymns, Scripture all remind us that a satisfactory Christology requires an understanding of discipleship which we would rather ignore for something more comfortable.